D1649102

RED ARROW

 INTERURBANS SPECIAL 96

RED ARROW

The First Hundred Years 1848-1948

By Ronald DeGraw

INTERURBAN PRESS
Glendale, California

Cover Painting by Larry Fisher

Front Endsheet:
Ivy covered most of the architectural details of 69th Street Terminal and the signal tower by 1916. An interurban car is departing from the terminal. Behind the interurban and the signal tower are three of the Lehigh Valley Transit Company's 800-series cars on the Philadelphia and Western, waiting to journey to Allentown. On the far right, next to the front door of the terminal, is a PRT Route 41 trolley, which ran to Front and Market Streets in Philadelphia from 1911 to 1920. Collection of Harry P. Albrecht

Rear Endsheet:
This poster showing service on all four of the company's rail routes was issued in 1933. Copies were placed in the stations. Collection of Ronald DeGraw

RED ARROW
The First Hundred Years 1848–1948

© 1985 Bryn Mawr Press, Inc.

All rights reserved. No part of this book may be used or reproduced without written permission from the publisher, except in the case of brief quotations used in reviews.

Published by
INTERURBAN PRESS
P. O. Box 6444
Glendale, California 91205

Manufactured in the United States of America

First Printing, 1985

Library of Congress Cataloging in Publication Data

DeGraw, Ronald, 1942–
  Red Arrow—the first 100 years.

  Bibliography: p.
  Includes index.
  1. Philadelphia Suburban Transportation Company—History.   I. Title.
HE4491.P6P823   1984   388.4′6′0974811   84-19748
ISBN 0-916374-67-X

To Karin Lance,

for her editorial assistance and
extraordinary tolerance,
this book is lovingly dedicated.

Acknowledgements

THE PHOTOGRAPHIC COMPREHENSIVENESS of this book was made possible by the generous assistance of Harry P. Albrecht, John J. Bowman, Jr., Stanley F. Bowman, Jr., David H. Cope, Harold E. Cox, William Crawford, Harre W. Demoro, E. Everett Edwards, William C. Janssen, Robert L. Long, Hilda Shadel Lucas, Andrew W. Maginnis, Fred W. Schneider, III, James P. Shuman, the late John Gibb Smith, Jr., Thomas Smith, Merritt H. Taylor, Jr., and Lester K. Wismer.

Mrs. Robert Johnston made available the Haverford Township Historical Society's Wilbur P. Hall Collection. David H. Cope printed the Wilbur Hall negatives.

John F. Calnan prepared all of the fine maps.

Photographs attributed to "PST" are from the files of the Philadelphia Suburban Transportation Company. All of these photographs together with more than 37,000 documents and other corporate records of PST form the "Red Arrow Lines Collection" at the Hagley Museum and Library (formerly the Eleutherian Mills Historical Library), in Greenville, Delaware. Grateful acknowledgement is due to Richmond D. Williams, Hagley's Deputy Director for Library Administration; Daniel Muir, head of Pictorial Collections and Audio Visual Services; and to Carol Hallman, Betty-Bright Low and Marjorie McNinch for their enthusiastic cooperation in making this material available for research and publication.

Grateful acknowledgement is also due Wendell J. Dillinger, whose college thesis written in the 1950s provided many details on the early history of Red Arrow.

Several ladies in large hats and a man in a bowler are waiting for a Collingdale car in the traction company's sparse waiting room. The doors on the right led into the PRT waiting room. (See chapter 3.) Collection of Harold E. Cox

Preface

THE STORY OF RED ARROW is one of remarkable business sagacity in an industry noteworthy for its many financial failures.

It's a fascinating tale that began when a group of farmers and merchants got together in 1848 to build a wooden toll road, and that went on to include an incredibly unsuccessful horsecar line, tiny steam dummy passenger cars that broke down more often than they ran, a meandering country trolley line where cars frequently jumped the track, and a speedy interurban that eventually evolved into a highly successful bus and rail network serving a large portion of Philadelphia's suburbs.

The success of the company came about because of three generations of men named Merritt Taylor.

When A. Merritt Taylor was only 24 years old in 1899, he managed to gain control of a faltering but potentially profitable country trolley line. He and his son, Merritt H. Taylor, and grandson, Merritt H. Taylor, Jr., controlled and expanded for 71 years a transportation system which came to include interurban rail lines, urban, suburban and intercity bus routes, and real estate ventures.

It was only through an act of the Pennsylvania Legislature that an end finally came to the extraordinarily successful Taylor transit empire.

This volume covers the first hundred years of the company's history, from its incorporation in 1848 until the postwar boom period of 1948. These were the formative years and the years of rapid and constant growth, the years of survival in the Great Depression because of bold decisions by the Taylors, and the boom times of World War II when ridership doubled within two years. As Red Arrow celebrated its centennial year, ridership reached the highest point in the company's history.

This volume is a revised, expanded version of a portion of *The Red Arrow,* which was published in 1972 and has been out of print for a decade.

A subsequent volume will cover the history of the Philadelphia and Western Railway from its incorporation in 1902 until its merger into Red Arrow in 1954.

A third volume will bring the story of Red Arrow, including the P&W, into the mid-1980s.

Contents

List of Maps

AN ACT

AUTHORIZING THE GOVERNOR TO INCORPORATE

THE

PHILADELPHIA AND WEST CHESTER

TURNPIKE ROAD COMPANY.

PHILADELPHIA:
MERRIHEW AND THOMPSON, PRINTERS,
No. 7 Carter's Alley.
1848.

Front cover of the legislation authorizing creation of the Philadelphia and West Chester Turnpike Road Company in 1848. PST

Chapter 1

Rotting Planks and Empty Horsecars, 1848–1891

A MERICAN TROOPS WERE FINISHING up a romantic war south of the Rio Grande, and James Polk was in the White House. Gold had been discovered in California, which was recently acquired from Mexico and not yet a state.

There were four million slaves in the South, and a group of belligerent ladies was meeting in Seneca Falls, New York, with the preposterous demand of equal rights for women.

It was 1848, and the United States of America was a mere 72 years old.

The steam locomotive had been around for less than two decades, and there was a railroad building boom going on. Local transportation within the cities was virtually nonexistent. There were some cabs, for those who could afford them, and there were a few overcrowded horse-drawn omnibus lines. The wealthy maintained their own carriages. The poor and the middle classes simply walked to work.

Streets were unbearably dusty or repulsively muddy. It would be nearly half a century before the trolley car became commonplace and another quarter century before the motor bus was practical.

It was in this setting that a group of farmers and merchants living west of Philadelphia decided to do something about their own local transportation problem, the miserably bumpy trail that ran from the city's edge westward to the little town of West Chester.

Philadelphia may have been America's Cradle of Liberty but at the time had only 120,000 residents. The boundaries of the city ran from the Delaware River to the Schuylkill River, and the main east-west road was Market Street. West of the Schuylkill was the Borough of West Philadelphia, a separate and sparsely settled municipality. Market Street continued through West Philadelphia to the Delaware County border at Cobbs Creek just west of 63rd Street. Then it ran another 20 miles to West Chester, which was the county seat of Chester County, and in this suburban portion it was called the West Chester Road.

This long dirt road was the main access to Philadelphia for the farmers and mill owners who lived west of the city. Several of these men got together in 1847, determined to improve the highway so that people and livestock would no longer get swallowed up by mud holes or caked with dust.

Most of Delaware County was then a wilderness, with only 4,205 families in the entire county. Upper Darby Township, most populous part of the county, boasted a mere 2,044 residents.

It was fashionable in those days to build turnpikes out of planks or stones, then charge tolls in order to make enough money for maintenance and a comfortable profit.

The prominent farmers and businessmen worked fast to carry out their idea, and by early 1848 they were able to submit to the Pennsylvania Legislature petitions with the names of 639 residents of Philadelphia and Delaware counties who favored the proposed West Chester turnpike.

Another 550 persons, who apparently didn't like the idea of having to pay to get into Philadelphia, opposed the road. But the legislature gave its approval on March 20, 1848, for a toll road from 42nd Street in West Philadelphia to Newtown Square, almost half the distance to West Chester. To aid the new Philadelphia and West Chester Turnpike Road Company, the legislature authorized the townships through which the road passed to purchase stock.

The Act of the legislature stipulated that the 10.5-mile road could be up to 60 feet wide and could be built out of "wood, stone or gravel, or any other hard substance well compacted together and of sufficient depth to secure a solid foundation." Grades were to be no more than five percent. Work on the road had to start in three years, with five miles completed within five years or the Act became void.

Tolls were to be one cent per mile for each horse or mule. But heavy wagons or stage coaches with three or more horses were charged one and a half cents per horse per mile on the theory that the heavier vehicles would do more damage to the turnpike.

If a person lied to a tolltaker about how far he had traveled, the Act called for a fine of $5; and if a toll collector tried to cheat a traveler, he could be fined $10, which was to be for "the use of the poor of the township in which the forfeiture is incurred."

Cattle, sheep and pigs, or people going to church or to a funeral, were exempt from the tolls.

Original petition submitted to the Pennsylvania Legislature, complaining that the West Chester Road is at certain times of the year "almost impassable" and asking that it be "turnpiked." PST

To the Honorable, the Senate and House of Representatives of the Commonwealth of Pennsylvania.

The Memorial of the undersigned Citizens of the Counties of Philadelphia, Delaware and Chester, and others, respectfully represents :—

That the West Chester Road, being one of the main thoroughfares leading to the City of Philadelphia, is traveled by so large a portion of the citizens of many of the Counties west of the river Schuylkill, that the traveling thereon, at certain seasons, is rendered difficult, and the state of the road almost impassable ; and, from the great amount of agricultural produce, from the highly improved, and still improving Counties of Delaware and Chester; and the raw material, and manufactured articles, going to and from the many manufactories, established in said Counties, as well as from the general increase of business and travel, that must necessarily pass over said road, it cannot be kept in suitable order and repair under the ordinary mode of repairing roads ; and, in the opinion of your petitioners, the traveling public, as well as those immediately along the line of the road, would be greatly benefited by having said road turnpiked, or bedded with some hard substance, sufficient to bear the burden passing over the same, and maintain a smooth and even surface. Your petitioners, therefore, humbly ask your Honorable Bodies to pass an Act authorizing the Governor to incorporate a Company to make an artificial road, on the bed of the West Chester Road, from the Western line of the Borough of West Philadelphia to the eleven mile stone, or Beaumont's Tavern, on said road, with such restrictions as will allow persons going to or from places of worship, or attending funerals with their vehicles and horses, and drovers with their cattle, to pass free.

If the company let the road get in poor condition, local magistrates could force the company to cease collecting tolls for that section until it was repaired. If a traveler purposely tried to avoid a toll gate, he could be fined $20. But if he was taken to court and then found not guilty, the company had to pay him $10.

Vandalism or littering was a $5 offense. Speeding was considered almost as serious a crime as it is today, and the Act provided for a $20 fine.

The Act declared: "All drivers and conductors of carts, wagons, and carriages of all kinds shall, except when passing by a vehicle or slower draught, keep their horses and carriages on the right hand side of the road in the passing direction, leaving the other side of the road free and clear for other carriages to pass and repass; and if any driver shall offend against this provision, he shall forfeit and pay any sum not exceeding five dollars...; and no driver of a carriage of any kind shall pass any other vehicle, going in the same direction, at a faster gait than a trot, at a rate not exceeding eight miles per hour, under a penalty of twenty dollars for each offense, one half to the use of the said Company, and the other half to the use of the informant."

In those days before speedometers and radar, it must have been difficult to know exactly when your horse was exceeding the eight-mile speed limit!

The Act was generous to the stockholders of the company, declaring that if the profits didn't produce a six percent dividend each year the tolls could be raised. But if the net income exceeded ten percent, the tolls would go down. The turnpike company never had to worry about reducing its tolls.

The Company Is Organized

The 41 commissioners named by the Act to sell the stock held their first meeting April 14, 1848, at John Hawkins' Black Horse Inn on the southeast corner of what is now West Chester Pike and Pennock Avenue in Upper Darby.

It took several months to round up subscriptions to 400 shares of stock. Finally the necessary list of subscribers was sent to the governor, who on January 23, 1849, issued orders officially approving the creation of the turnpike company.

Most of the early meetings were held at the Black Horse Inn, and the first stockholders' meeting took place February 21, 1849. Abraham L. Pennock, an inventor, a manufacturer of mailbags for the post office and the manager of several estates along the West Chester Road, was elected president and John Sellers was named treasurer. Both were Quakers.

The Sellers family were early settlers in the Philadelphia area. Samuel Sellers and his brother, George, had come to America from England in 1682 and purchased a 100-acre tract from William Penn eight years later in what is now Upper Darby Township and Millbourne Borough.

George Sellers was killed by Indians, but his brother went on to head a family that ultimately owned large tracts of land and several mills along Cobbs Creek. Samuel, a weaver, settled along the West Chester Road at Cobbs Creek in Millbourne and built the first twisting mill in America for making thread.

John Sellers, grandson to Samuel, further expanded the Millbourne site and before he died in 1804 there was a cloth mill, a flour mill, a mill to grind gypsum, another for spices, a sawmill and a "tilting mill" which manufactured farm tools.

In 1814 his son, also named John, built a new flour mill and installed the first turbine wheel in the industry. John Sellers, Jr., introduced steam power in 1876. The big Millbourne Mills was finally torn down in 1927 to make way for a Sears Roebuck department store.

Both Pennock and Sellers as well as the 12 other members of the board of managers of the company had great personal interest in the development of the area along the turnpike.

The initial question facing the managers when they held their first meeting March 5, 1849, was what sort of material to use to build the road. They quickly decided that planks "would be the best, most pleasant and economical road and would be most advantageous to the stockholders."

According to contemporary reports, roads made out of hemlock cost only one-third as much as stone roads. And the hemlock was supposed to last seven years, putting maintenance costs also at about one-third of what they would have been with stone. So it didn't take the managers long to decide on planks.

They had made a bad decision, but it would take them several years to find that out. The company had a difficult time obtaining planks during

Shares of turnpike stock were quickly sold, at $25 each. This is the first page of the company's first stock subscription book. John Sellers was one of the initial purchasers. PST

the latter part of 1849, and so construction was delayed until the following spring. A contract to build the first three miles of road was signed April 10, 1850, and David George, one of the managers, was chosen to supervise the project.

The first three-mile section of the road was completed October 10. Under the Act creating the company, the courts had to appoint viewers to inspect and approve each three-mile section before tolls could be collected. George apparently wasn't taking any chances, for he made sure that after the inspection tour the viewers were treated to a hearty dinner, which cost the company $8.

The first tolls were collected October 12, 1850, with two toll gates. One, operated by William Davy, whom the company paid 75 cents a day, was located between 44th and 45th Streets near the eastern end of the turnpike. The second gate was near 62nd Street.

In those days before credit cards, regular customers were allowed to pay their bills to the tollkeepers only once a week, which was later extended to once a month.

Market Street through Philadelphia and West Philadelphia was paved only as far as 40th Street, leaving a gap of about two blocks of unpaved road between 40th Street and the new turnpike. The turnpike managers believed this condition was detrimental to traffic, so they loaned the Borough of West Philadelphia $9,000 to pave the two blocks with stone.

The following February the managers decided to begin construction on the second three miles of roadway. This would carry the turnpike west to Manoa, approximately where Eagle Road now crosses West Chester Pike.

This time, however, the company took charge of most of the construction itself instead of hiring a contractor. Laborers were paid 87½ cents a day to work on the road, and again there was difficulty in securing enough lumber.

There also was trouble with the Black Horse Hill just west of Garrett Road. Building the turnpike to conform with the desired three-degree gradient was difficult, and for this an outside contracting firm was hired. The firm built a temporary road on adjacent properties while the obstinate hill was properly graded.

The road was finished October 23, 1851, and court-appointed viewers

John Sellers, also known as John Sellers, Jr., was influential in the company's affairs for more than half a century. He was a prominent Delaware County businessman, controlling the large Millbourne Mills. Historical Society of Pennsylvania

Receipt issued to John Sellers for the first installment payment on his 20 shares of stock. Dates shown on most of the company's early records are written in Quaker style, since most of the early officials were members of the Society of Friends. PST

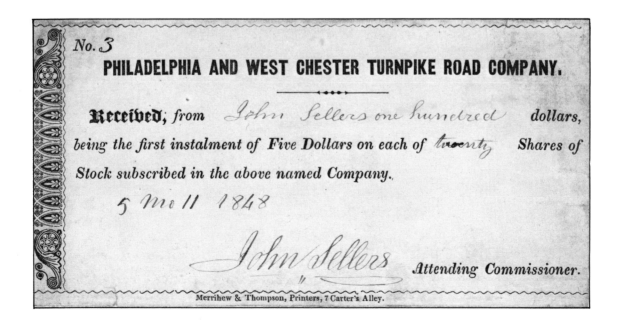

No. 3

PHILADELPHIA AND WEST CHESTER TURNPIKE ROAD COMPANY.

Received, from *John Sellers one hundred* dollars,

being the first instalment of Five Dollars on each of *twenty* Shares of

Stock subscribed in the above named Company.

5 Mo 11 1848

John Sellers   Attending Commissioner.

Merrihew & Thompson, Printers, 7 Carter's Alley.

approved it the same day. Toll collecting began the following day.

The toll gate near 62nd Street was abolished and a new one built at the intersection with Garrett Road in Upper Darby.

In his first annual report to the board of managers on December 31, 1851, George mentions several drainage problems and portions of the road which had washed out. These problems continued at various spots along the road as long as the planks remained. During some particularly heavy storms, whole sections of the road floated on an inch or two of water due to washouts and poor drainage. George noted in his report that a total of $5,571 in tolls had been collected during 1851.

Completion to Manoa left the road only 4.5 miles short of Newtown Square, and preliminary steps were taken late in 1852 to begin another extension. James Miller, a stockholder in the company, was chosen to engineer the road, and construction began from Newtown Square eastward in February 1853.

Two and a half miles were ready for the viewers on September 7, and tolls began to be collected shortly afterward.

This left only a two-mile gap from Manoa westward still to be finished, but this was the most difficult portion since it involved several hills and required a great deal of excavation.

Two different contractors walked off the job after arguments with Miller, but the road was finally finished and examined by viewers on November 23. Tolls started coming in three days later.

A third toll gate was set up between Springfield Road and Media Line Road, about two miles from the western end of the turnpike.

The entire 10.5-mile road had been built with two tracks, as a lane of plank road was called. Each track was eight feet wide and they were separated by a narrow strip of dirt.

Building double-track through sparsely populated territory was a great mistake, as the managers soon found out. Most turnpike companies of the era built only one track in outlying areas, and when two vehicles met one would have to pull off the road to permit the other to pass.

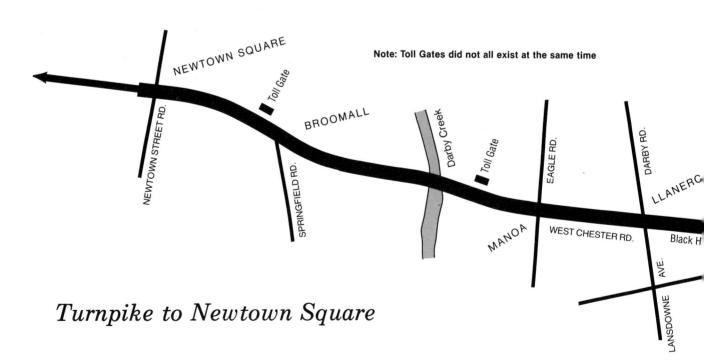

Turnpike to Newtown Square

Some stockholders had cautioned against building two tracks west of Manoa, but their warnings went unheeded. Even William Worrell, when he was the company's president in 1852, warned against double-track, claiming it would be "exceedingly unwise and unnecessary."

"Nearly all the travel on that part, during particular periods of each day, is in the same direction, either east or west," said Worrell in a report to the stockholders. "The anticipated inconvenience, in the case of a single-track, from the supposed frequent meeting of vehicles, is not, therefore, likely to be realized."

Worrell predicted the two tracks would decay quicker than the amount of traffic would wear them out.

The Act of the legislature had stipulated double-track, and there was a half-hearted attempt by the managers to have this amended. But after considerable protest from residents along the line, any further thought of single-tracking the section was abandoned.

Construction of the entire road had cost $72,000, which had been raised completely through the sale of 2,985 shares of $25 stock sold mainly to farmers and businessmen living in the area.

Good Profits—For A While

For the first few years the company managed to pay very nice dividends. The rate was six percent in 1851, 10 percent in 1852 and 1853 and eight percent in 1854. But by 1855 it dipped to only three percent, and the meager profits for the year didn't even equal that much.

A catastrophe had occurred. Much of the hemlock on the eastern part of the turnpike had deteriorated so badly that it needed immediate replacing. Despite authoritative estimates that the life of hemlock was seven years, half the planks in the first three miles had to be replaced and the other half had to be turned over. Part of the road by mid-1855 was in very bad shape, and the managers decided to replace the hemlock with black oak. It was twice as expensive, but it was supposed to last 12 years.

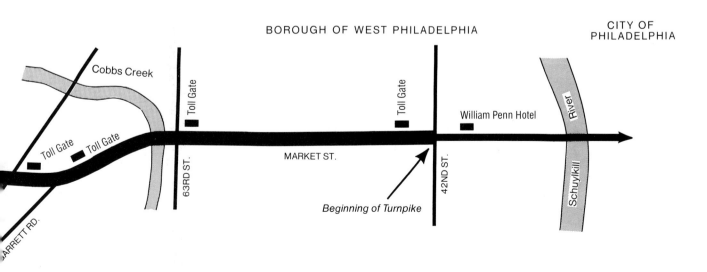

Map by John F. Calnan

Gatekeepers at each of the toll gates turned in their revenues once a week to the company's treasurer, who in 1855 was John Sellers. Receipts for Gate No. 1 for the week ending December 1, 1855, were $94.57, from which the gatekeeper deducted his wages of $8.
PST

The company got the legislature to approve a weight limitation of 1,600 pounds for vehicles with tires less than four inches wide and 2,000 pounds for vehicles with wider tires. It was thought that heavy loads had contributed to the deterioration of the planks.

So concerned were the managers about offering at least a six percent annual dividend, and so high were the maintenance bills growing, that the company sought legislative permission to tear up one of the tracks. It would be relaid, the managers promised, if and when dividends exceeded

Philadelphia and West Chester Turnpike Road Company.

GATE No. 1, *December 4* 1855

This Certifies that I have paid the Treasurer of the Company the Tolls collected at this Gate for the week ending *December 1 1855* being *Ninety four* Dollars 57 Cents, $ 94.57

And received of him my wages for the same period, being *Eight* 100 Dollars. 8.00

Balance, $ 86.57

Countersigned,

John Sellers Treasurer. *Thomas K. Hall* Collector.

Wm. Birney, Printer, 22 South Third Street.

Philadelphia and West Chester Turnpike Road Company.

GATE No. 1, *Dec 2nd* 1878

This Certifies that I have paid the Treasurer of the Company the Tolls collected at this Gate for the week ending *Nov 30th 1878* being *Ninety One* Dollars 00 Cents, $ 91.00

And received of him my wages for the same period, being *10.00* 100 Dollars. 10.00

Countersigned,

Balance, $ 81.00

Joseph Seedom Treasurer. *Peter K. Bloom Sr.* Collector.

FRIENDS' BOOK ASSOCIATION OF PHILADELPHIA, 706 ARCH ST.

Twenty-three years later Gate No. 1 was still producing about the same amount in weekly tolls, although the gatekeeper's wages had risen to $10.
PST

six percent. The legislature concurred, and one track of the roadway between Cobbs Creek and Newtown Square was ripped up, even though part of it had been installed only two years earlier. The original double-track was retained in West Philadelphia because of the greater amount of traffic there.

The best of the planks torn up were used to repair the remaining track. But the managers soon suffered an even greater financial blow when they learned that the black oak planks were actually inferior to the original hemlock, and by 1858 it was estimated that 377,000 feet of new planks would have to be purchased each year just to keep the road in good shape.

Because of all the problems with the planks, the company experimented in 1856 with stone, converting a 400-foot stretch of road. By the end of 1858 a mile of the turnpike had been changed from planks to stone, and consideration was given to changing the entire western end of the road to stone to replace the planks.

The company sold many of the old planks at the rate of about 300 for $9, and a total of $130 was obtained during 1860 from the sale of old planks. By 1865 as much as $8,000 a year was being spent for stone.

Total receipts for 1860 were $11,730, with Toll Gate No. 1 being by far the most lucrative of the three. This left the company with a cash balance on January 1, 1861, of $3,776, which Adam C. Eckfeldt, then the president, declared was a "handsome surplus." Half of it was quickly gotten rid of by declaring another stock dividend.

A New Technology

While the turnpike company was trying to solve the case of the decaying hemlock, at least two other men had their sights on an entirely different type of transportation for the West Chester Road.

E. Spencer Miller, a Philadelphia attorney, had gotten a bill passed by the legislature creating the Delaware County Passenger Rail Road Company. It was signed into law March 29, 1859, and authorized construction of a rail line along Market Street and the West Chester Turnpike from

Toll Gate No. 2, located at State Road, provided living quarters for the gatekeeper and his family. Collection of John Gibb Smith, Jr.

about 41st Street to Newtown Square, "as far from time to time as the public convenience may require or the public use may justify."

Railroad cars were to have the right-of-way and anyone interfering with their plodding progress could be fined $5 to $10.

A year earlier James Miller, who had been the engineer for the western portion of the turnpike, attempted to convince the West Philadelphia Passenger Railway to extend its line out the turnpike. He had been a founder of the horsecar line built from 41st Street to downtown Philadelphia. The turnpike managers approved the plan, but the horsecar company turned it down and built northward into more populous sections of the city instead.

The Borough of West Philadelphia had been abolished in 1854 and the whole area between the Schuylkill River and Cobbs Creek, near 63rd Street, was made part of the city of Philadelphia. James Miller was named surveyor for this territory, and he saw the horsecar line as a good way to develop the area. Philadelphia's first horsecar line—the Frankford and Southwark Passenger Railroad—opened January 20, 1858.

The two Millers, who do not appear to have been related, were named together with eight other men as commissioners to organize the newly created Delaware County Passenger Rail Road. Most of the 10 were associated with the turnpike company, including Sellers, Pennock, A. Lewis Smith, who later became counsel for the turnpike; James P. Afflick, owner of the Spread Eagle Tavern in Manoa, and Joseph Powell, who would soon become president of the turnpike.

Gate No. 5 was located on the north side of West Chester Pike between Springfield Road and Media Line Road in Larchmont. Gatekeepers were on duty for 24 hours a day. At night, the pole between the front door and the large tree was swung across the road to prevent travelers from passing without paying a toll. The pole was called a "pike," and travelers called to the gatekeeper to "turn the pike" so they could get through. PST

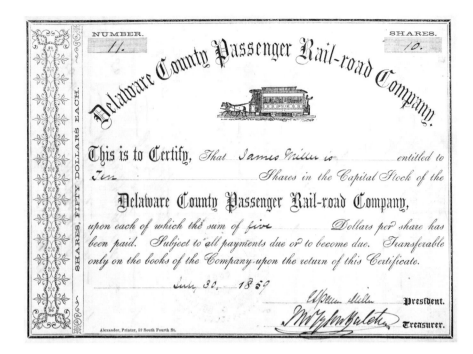

James Miller, one of the organizers of the horsecar line, had enough confidence in it to invest $500 in 10 shares of stock. The stock certificate is signed by E. Spencer Miller, the company's first president. Collection of Harold E. Cox

The 300 shares of stock necessary to get the official approval of the governor were quickly sold—largely to stockholders of the turnpike company—and the first shareholders' meeting was held in June 1859. Spencer Miller was elected president.

The next month the turnpike managers granted to the railroad perpetual right-of-way over the West Chester Road. The contract said the railroad could lay a single-track in the southern plank track and that the railroad would maintain this plank track in good condition.

It was decided to initially build four miles of line from approximately 41st Street to the Howard House at Pennock Avenue in Upper Darby.

Built in 1810, the Howard House was a well-known temperance inn and was owned by Sellers, a staunch prohibitionist and abolitionist. It was just across the street from the Black Horse Inn and it stood until the early 1970s, when it was torn down to create a parking lot for an adjacent pizza restaurant.

Meetings of the turnpike company were shifted to the Howard House in 1860, and until the Civil War the hotel was a frequent stop for slaves on the "underground railroad" route to freedom.

The first construction contract for the railway went to Parks, Simpson and Company on September 26, 1859, which built the entire four miles of line in the remarkably short time of less than two and a half months.

The track consisted of 18⅔-pound strap rail on top of white oak stringers, supported by ties four feet apart. The track gauge was 5 feet 2½ inches and hemlock plank was laid on the ties between the rails to provide a walkway for the horses.

The horsecars began their trip at a siding on the grounds of the William Penn Hotel at 3811 Market Street, where there were stables for the horses. Then they ran for nearly three blocks over the double-track West Philadelphia Passenger Railway under a trackage rights agreement before reaching the single-track route of the Delaware County Passenger Rail Road. There were few sidings along the four-mile suburban line because there were seldom more than two cars in operation at the same time.

E. Spencer Miller was president of the horsecar company from 1859 until shortly before it was abandoned in 1865. Historical Society of Pennsylvania

The first schedule of the Delaware County line appeared as a small advertisement in the "Philadelphia Public Ledger" on December 30, 1859. The original ad was a mere 3/8" by 2-1/8" and was buried on a page filled with classified ads. Collection of Ronald DeGraw

There were also stables to accommodate the railway's motive power at the Howard House.

Problems occurred even before service began. Although the line was finished in early December, the two horsecars which had been ordered were not expected to arrive until the following February.

This dilemma was finally solved by leasing two cars from the West Philadelphia line, with service beginning December 22, 1859. Originally a car left each terminal every hour from 7 a.m. until 10 p.m. Mondays through Saturdays. No horsecars ran anywhere in Philadelphia on Sundays because of the strict "blue laws" in force at the time.

Patronage didn't justify the hourly service, and within a month three trips had been eliminated.

In 1863 the leasing arrangement with the West Philadelphia line was terminated, and the suburban horsecars ended their runs where they connected with the city cars at 41st Street.

Despite the dearth of patronage, the company had bought four cars by the end of 1860 and a fifth the following year. But by the end of operations the roster was again down to only two cars. Despite the obviously light patronage that was anticipated, the cars were built for two-horse, two-man operation. Possibly the company could have survived longer if it had used the recently invented lightweight one-horse, one-man cars.

In 1862 the company owned as many as 16 horses, but that number dwindled over the next couple of years.

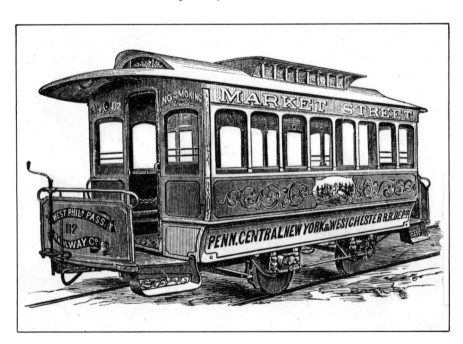

The Delaware County Passenger Rail Road operated cars similar to this one owned by the West Philadelphia Passenger Railway. Historical Society of Pennsylvania

Light was provided for the little cars at night by oil lamps, but the method of obtaining the oil may have been unique. Instead of maintaining a large supply, the company forced the conductors to stop and buy small amounts of it from local farmers or stores whenever a car's supply ran low. The conductors deducted the cost of the fuel from their day's receipts.

Two sleighs were purchased by the line shortly after it opened, although there is no record of them ever having been used. The sleighs were gone by the time service was abandoned.

The promoters of the horsecar line had high hopes for it, and they

Both the Delaware County line and the West Philadelphia line operated heavy two-horse, two-man cars. This view was taken at 65th and Vine Streets in West Philadelphia in 1866. Haverford Township Historical Society

definitely expected to eventually extend all the way to Newtown Square. They even considered the possibility of hauling freight on the line at night.

"We believe the day will come when the cars of the Delaware County Passenger Rail Road will become comforts and conveniences to those along its route as ordinary and necessary as passenger cars now are in the city, when its stock will be a safe and productive investment, and when those who have treated us so unkindly and illiberally will see their error, and perhaps regret their course," declared the first annual report of the railroad.

It was referring to the pronounced lack of enthusiasm by residents of the area in purchasing stock in the railroad. Company officials carried on a vigorous promotional campaign, but all they could raise was $20,000 in stock subscriptions, about $10,000 less than the four-mile line had cost to build.

The Beginning of the End

It was then that the company took the fatal step that would eventually force its death. Seven percent mortgage bonds totaling $10,000 were offered, but even most of these couldn't be sold. Finally, after offering a generous discount, about $5,000 was produced by the bonds.

Most of them had been sold to E. Spencer Miller, who had a great deal of faith in the future of the line, and to William Parks, who had very little faith in it. Parks was head of Parks, Simpson and Company, which had built the line, and he finally agreed to take bonds in part payment only if he could get a discount and if Miller would agree to join him in foreclosure proceedings whenever the company defaulted on payments of interest or principal.

As it turned out, the financial condition of the company was generally so bad that Parks was one of the very few bondholders who ever received any interest. Finally there wasn't enough money to pay even him.

The railroad's business turned out to be very seasonal in nature, but even the heavy summer ridership was insufficient to offset the losses

The Howard House, a temperance inn owned by John Sellers and located on the northwest corner of West Chester Pike and Pennock Avenue in Upper Darby, was the western terminal for the horsecar line and the scene of many of the meetings held by the horsecar company and the turnpike company. Collection of Hilda Shadel Lucas

OPPOSITE:

Horsecar Line, 1859–1865

sustained during the winter. The first year produced a deficit of $399 after interest on the bonds. Revenues of $5,158 had failed to match expenses of $5,557.

The next year's loss was $400, and the inflation accompanying the Civil War drove expenses higher each year.

Spencer Miller desperately appointed a committee to try to work out a solution to the financial problems, and the committee concluded that "if the cost of repairing the plank track was taken off of the company, and the expenses of running lessened to one-half in the winter season, the road could be sustained and the interest paid; without these, we must cease running and wind up."

This was in 1861, only a year and a half after operations had begun.

Miller did his best to convince the managers of the turnpike company to abolish the requirement that forced the horsecar company to repair the plank track that its cars used. But the managers—who by this time probably realized the line would never amount to much financially—refused to pay any attention to him.

Finally in 1864 the turnpike managers agreed to remove the restriction if the railroad would reimburse it for repairs to the planks with bonds taking preference over those already issued. Strong objections from the railroad's bondholders killed that idea, and the turnpike officials weren't the least bit interested in an offer to be paid with bonds of the series already outstanding.

Early in 1864 there appeared one faint glimmer of hope, and the railroad company tried to grasp it. The previous November, the Frankford and Southwark Passenger Railroad Company, operating in the northern part of the city, had placed in regular service an unusual steam-powered passenger car named *Alpha*. This steam dummy, not much bigger than a horsecar, had been running experimentally over several of the city's street railway lines and was finally deemed successful enough for regular service.

The Delaware County Rail Road officials saw in the *Alpha* a way to save money because horses wouldn't have to be maintained and fed the year-round, even when they weren't producing any revenue.

The railroad went to the legislature, and on May 24, 1864, got permission to run the steam dummies if the turnpike managers sanctioned them.

Miller pleaded with the managers, but they refused to permit the steam dummies to run on the West Chester Road. Possibly the managers feared that the unusual vehicles would scare horses as they chugged along the turnpike, particularly on the single-track section of the road.

Miller had been defeated again, but he refused to give up. Once more he attempted to attract new investors to the railroad, and once more he met with complete failure. While everybody around him clearly saw that the line was doomed, Miller refused to admit it. The line was hauling 300 to 400 riders a day, and Miller thought that, given a few years, it could begin to show a profit.

By 1864 the plank road on which the railroad ran was in extremely bad condition, chiefly because the railroad just didn't have the money to make the needed repairs. Although the original agreement with the turnpike company permitting the railroad to construct its line decreed that the railroad would make all repairs to the plank road, there were no penalties listed in the event the repairs weren't made.

So in mid-1864 the turnpike managers considered buying the railroad. A. Lewis Smith, attorney for the turnpike, said he didn't think they had the legal right to buy a railroad, so the managers came up with another plan. They would buy up enough of the railroad's bonds so they could foreclose. Both Spencer Miller and Parks had agreed to sell their bonds.

But again Smith said he doubted it would be legal. The turnpike, Smith thought, should seek the approval of the legislature before buying any bonds.

The legislature gave its approval in March 1865 to a bill permitting the turnpike not only to buy the bonds of the railroad but to also purchase the entire railroad company and its franchises if they were offered for sale at an auction.

This meant the turnpike could now buy the bonds, institute foreclosure proceedings, then buy the company at auction.

The legislature went even further. The turnpike company could remove the tracks of the railroad, the bill said, but it failed to mention what would happen to the franchises if there were no longer a railroad operating.

While the turnpike managers were busy with the legislature, Parks decided he had waited long enough for the interest payments on his bonds. He had gotten interest for only two and a half of the five years, so he wrote to Spencer Miller reminding him of the agreement Miller had made to help Parks foreclose. Miller remembered, and in January 1865 he stepped down from the presidency of the embattled little line, to be succeeded by James Miller.

Several other bondholders at this time also began demanding their money. The trustees of the bonds, Sellers and Powell, notified James Miller on April 6 that they would "take possession of the property under the powers contained in the mortgage" and would sell it at auction.

By this time the little horsecars had stopped running, service having ended in March 1865. The auction took place May 3 at the Howard House, and up for bids were four miles of single-track, two horsecars, three horses and some harnesses. The turnpike managers purchased the line for $4,100, which was distributed to the bondholders. Stockholders got nothing.

Some of the turnpike officials were seriously interested in reopening the railroad, and a committee was named "to consider and propose efficient measures to put the railroad track in good order for both common

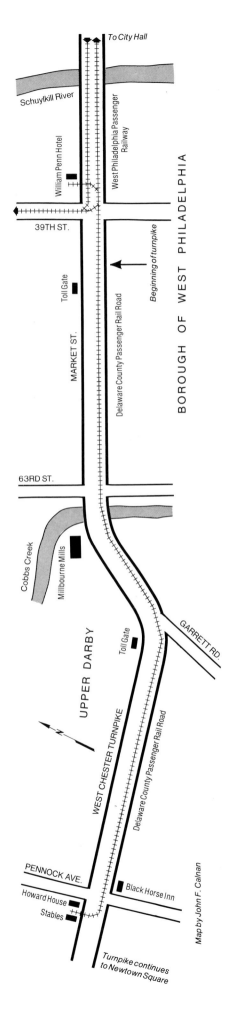

and railroad travel and that the same committee be authorized to run the cars on the railroad temporarily."

But the cars never ran again, and the inevitable decision to rip up the tracks was soon made. It was inevitable because the turnpike company just didn't have any money at the time. The company was right in the middle of a big and expensive project to replace the unsuccessful planks with stone.

The two Millers and others interested in rehabilitating the railroad met in the Howard House on July 14. One plan proposed would have cost about $8,000 for repairs. Another more elaborate scheme called for rebuilding with heavy 47-pound rail at a cost of $40,000, more than the original construction bill had amounted to.

This meeting even went so far as to appoint a committee to solicit stock subscriptions for the proposed venture. But the committee, like everything else connected with the railroad, met with failure, managing to come up with a mere $3,182 in stock pledges.

In August the turnpike company removed the iron from the railroad and sold it to the Brooklyn and Canarsie Rail Road Company for $5,118, making a $1,018 profit on the deal. Powell bought the three horses and was put in charge of selling the horsecars.

But still the dream of a railroad was not dead.

The following January a committee of seven managers was named to sell additional turnpike stock so that the railroad could be rebuilt. After a month, however, they had raised only $4,500, and everybody finally admitted the railroad was a hopeless idea. The last remains of the horsecar line were ripped up in the summer of 1867.

The Pike Hangs On

While the railroad was dying, the turnpike was pouring forth all the money it could muster to make sure it, too, didn't die. Tons of crushed stone were bought to repave the road west of Cobbs Creek. The job was completed to Newtown Square in 1867, with most of the stone coming from the small quarries dotting the turnpike.

This left only the eastern portion of the road, within the city limits, still built of planks. Both plank tracks here had deteriorated badly, but the company decided to keep the planks instead of converting to stone. New planking was laid between the eastern terminus and 60th Street in 1867.

The managers probably decided to retain the planks within the city because they expected to lose this portion of their toll road eventually, since the city was slowly beginning to expand westward.

An Act to "open, pave and grade Market Street between 43rd and 63rd Streets" was passed by the legislature in 1870 with the implication that the turnpike should be turned over to the city of Philadelphia. The Act provided no compensation for the company, yet the managers for some reason failed to contest it. After stockholder approval, the road east of Cobbs Creek was given to the city on August 20, 1872, and Toll Gate No. 1 was discontinued that night. A formal deed was signed with the city August 29.

The toll house at Garrett Road was renumbered No. 1, and a new house —No. 2—was built just east of Darby Creek, half a mile west of Manoa. Another toll house was added at State Road halfway up the Black Horse Hill in 1879. Several temporary little toll shacks were put up at various locations at different times when it was found that people were trying to circumvent the regular toll gates.

The loss of the portion of the turnpike within the city left the company with a well-paved 8.5-mile stone toll road from Cobbs Creek to Newtown Square.

In the Civil War years, with the road reduced to single-track west of Cobbs Creek, dividends of between two and five percent a year had been possible. But wages spiraled upward during the war, from $19 a month for a laborer in 1860 to $28 a month by 1865. Wages of the toll collectors

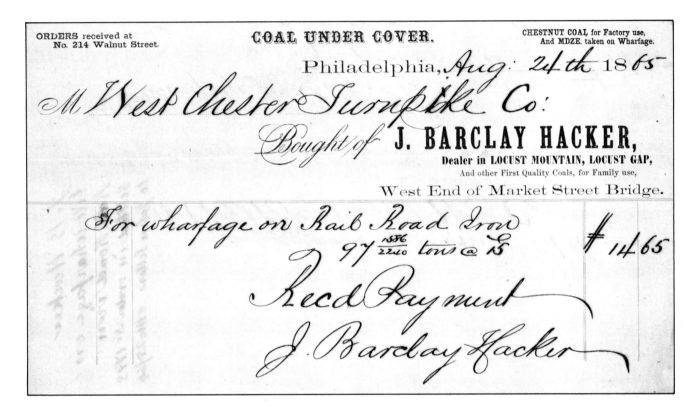

The turnpike company removed the iron rail from the horsecar line in August 1865 and sold it to the Brooklyn and Canarsie Rail Road Company. This is the invoice for the wharfage of the iron pending its shipment to Brooklyn. PST

1891.

NEWTOWN AND PHILADELPHIA STAGE.

SUMMER ARRANGEMENTS.

During the months of April, May, June, July, August and September,

The Stage will run on Monday, Wednesday, Thursday and Saturday of each week as follows:

Will leave Newtown Square at **7.15** A. M.; Broomall, **7.40** A. M.; Manoa, **8.05** A. M.; Upper Darby, **8.35** A. M.   Arriving at Wm. Penn Hotel at **9.15** A. M.

Returning: Will leave Wm. Penn Hotel, 38th and Market Streets, at **4.15** P. M.; Upper Darby, **5.00** P. M.; Manoa, **5.30** P. M.; Broomall, **6.05** P. M.   Arriving at Newtown Square at **6.30** P. M.

SINGLE FARES, - - - 50, 40, 30 and 10 Cents.

Round Trip Fares, made the same day, will be reduced to **75, 60** and **45 Cents** west of Upper Darby.

Baggage and Express Packages of all kinds (except liquor) will be carried and taken or sent to all parts of the City at reasonable rates.

Smoking, as well as spitting on the floor of the Coach, is positively forbidden.

I will only be responsible for packages given to my care. Packages belonging to passengers will be carried at their risk.

Extra fare will be charged for service other than regular trip.

(OVER)   **WM. F. SNITE, Proprietor.**

William Snite's stage coaches offered only a single round trip daily between Newtown Square and Philadelphia before the trolley line was opened in 1895. Round-trip fares were 75 cents. At 38th and Market Streets, stage passengers had to transfer to horsecars to reach downtown Philadelphia. PST rose 40 percent during the same period, so the company hiked the toll rate in January 1864 from one cent per horse per mile to a cent and a half.

Right after the war the company had the highest revenues of its history so far, with $14,314 in 1866 and $14,287 in 1867. It was found necessary in 1867, however, to sell $7,000 in additional bonds, and no dividends were paid until the bonds were retired four years later.

A further toll increase to two cents a mile occurred December 1, 1870, and then for 10 of the 11 years beginning in 1871 dividends totaled 50 percent of the par value of the stock.

Another rehabilitation of the highway beginning in 1882 again forced the company into debt. New bonds totaling $24,800 were issued, and although the project was costly it put the road in the best shape ever. The second track was rebuilt from Cobbs Creek to Darby Creek to handle the increased traffic, and the original track was widened to 15 feet and reconstructed to the best standards of the time.

In 1888, Wilmer Broadbelt, who had for the past two years been in charge of sprinkling the road in the summer to keep the dust down, offered to maintain the entire turnpike. Previously, local residents had been hired from time to time to supply the needed stone and labor for repairs.

The managers immediately accepted Broadbelt's offer and even bought a stone crusher for him to use. Broadbelt supplied all the wagons, men and supervision to keep the road in repair, and he continued to sprinkle it. This arrangement lasted until 1892.

The only form of public transportation along the West Chester Road in those early days was William Snite's stage coach, which ran from Newtown Square to the William Penn Hotel at 38th and Market Streets in the mornings and back out again at night. The journey took two hours each way, and a round-trip ticket cost 75 cents.

Newtown Square was by far the oldest of the many small towns along the pike. In fact, it was the first inland town laid out by William Penn in 1681. Penn called it Central Square and he conceived of a dream town which was never built.

At that time the area was wilderness inhabited by Indians and there wasn't even a highway connecting it with Philadelphia. In 1699, Penn ordered a road to be built, and people gradually began moving out into the area. Newtown Square received its first post office in 1828, and the stage coaches began carrying the mail.

For more than a century, stage coaches had plied the West Chester Road. In 1800, the stage ran out to West Chester one day and back into Philadelphia the next, offering triweekly service at the exorbitant one-way fare of $1.25.

But a new form of transportation was soon going to make the slow stage coaches obsolete.

Chapter 2

Trolleys on the Turnpike, 1892–1898

SINCE HE HAD BEEN A SMALL BOY, John N.M. Shimer had dreamed of building a railroad along the West Chester Road to his birthplace at Castle Rock, two miles west of Newtown Square.

Shimer spent his youth at Castle Rock, and his father's mill required that someone in the family make daily trips to Philadelphia. Young Shimer had gone along on many of these trips, and he had been fascinated by the little horsecars which meandered as far west as the Howard House in Upper Darby.

He had managed to ride the line several times, and when it was sold at auction in 1865 the 15-year-old Shimer was there.

After he married and moved to Philadelphia, Shimer went into the scrap iron business. He became a partner with L. & R. Wister and Company, iron and steel merchants, where he often dealt with railroad officials. In 1888 he became vice president of Choctaw Coal and Railway Company, which planned to build a railroad from Little Rock, Arkansas, to Albuquerque, New Mexico.

About the same time—in the late 1880s—he started buying up as much stock of the turnpike company as he could. The company wasn't paying dividends then, so stock was selling for less than $3 a share.

Shimer had several friends buy stock also, but none of them had the stock transferred to their names on the company's books. This permitted Shimer to become a major stockholder without the knowledge of the company's officers.

Late in 1891, when he thought he had enough stock, he went to see John Sellers, Jr., and convinced him to go along with the dream of resurrecting the railway. The Sellers family still held a major block of the turnpike stock.

Shimer felt the old franchise of the Delaware County Passenger Rail Road Company was still valid, and that the turnpike company still owned the franchise because it had purchased the horsecar line. It was on the basis of this franchise that Shimer was confident that he could legally rebuild the railroad as an electric trolley line.

A few months after his meeting with Sellers, Shimer learned that a Chester, Pennsylvania, man named John Dyer was also planning to incorporate a railroad to run along the turnpike. If the old horsecar franchise was still valid, then Dyer could not legally build on the turnpike. But if it wasn't valid and Dyer built first, Shimer would be in trouble.

Shimer hadn't yet been able to determine for certain whether the 33-year-old franchise was still good, and he wasn't taking any chances. So he incorporated the Philadelphia, Castle Rock and West Chester Railway Company on December 14, 1892. The company's charter gave it the right

A drawing of the Battle of Llanerch Crossing appeared in the "Philadelphia Times" on July 18, 1895. Pennsylvania Railroad employees have ripped out the trolley crossing, and the railroad man on the right stands guard with a rifle. A steam dummy sits on the hill, with the Llanerch toll house in the upper left. The dispute was finally resolved in the traction company's favor. Collection of Ronald DeGraw

to build a passenger railway along the turnpike from 63rd Street to Newtown Square, then further along the West Chester Road to Ridley Creek, five miles west of Newtown Square.

Shimer tried to get the right to also have this company build along Market Street in the city, but by this time the West Philadelphia Passenger Railway had extended its line as far west as 63rd and Market Streets.

Shimer desperately wanted his railroad to go all the way to 38th and Market Streets, just as the old horsecar line had done. For the next several years he waged a complicated legal battle which he ultimately lost. To start with, Shimer had Charles S. Hinchman, a turnpike stockholder and a proponent of the railway idea, ask the state attorney general for a ruling that the railway franchise had expired. According to the 1849 law under which the horsecar line had been incorporated, its franchise would expire two years after the railroad ceased operating, which would have been 1867.

But the attorney general replied: "I am by no means satisfied that . . . the company complained of has forfeited its charter, but whether it has or not is a question which . . . I am of the opinion can be raised upon a proceeding instituted by your stockholders in a court of equity."

Hinchman then, on the advice of Shimer, asked Delaware County Common Pleas Court to declare that the railway franchise acquired by the turnpike was void. But the judge replied that an individual stockholder could not obtain a forfeiture of a franchise.

Shimer wanted to try again just to make sure, so he had Hinchman appeal his case to the state Supreme Court in early 1894.

The Supreme Court decreed just what Shimer wanted to hear: "The Act of 1865 . . . expressly authorized those things to be done which, ordinarily, would be regarded as evidence of an intention to abandon. When the turnpike company sold the cars, horses, harness, rails and iron formerly belonging to the railroad company, they did so in pursuance of an express legislative authority, and incurred thereby no implication of abandonment. The franchise of the railroad continued, and may therefore be resumed at pleasure."

In other words, if the turnpike company had simply purchased the

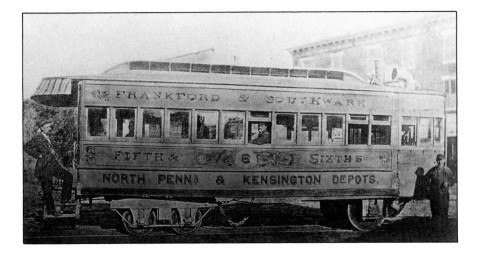

Steam dummies went into service on the Frankford and Southwark Passenger Railroad Company in the 1860s. Nine of them were purchased by the traction company in July 1895. Collection of Ronald DeGraw

horsecar line in 1865—as some of the managers had wanted to do—instead of seeking a special Act of the legislature authorizing them to acquire it, then the franchise would now be void.

Even while the case was still before the Supreme Court, Shimer ordered a short stretch of track laid along the turnpike at Llanerch and another small section just west of 63rd Street. The two tiny pieces of track were Shimer's hope of blocking the mighty Pennsylvania Railroad, which had been fiercely battling the upstart trolley companies wherever it encountered them—and usually winning.

The Pennsylvania Railroad was building a branch from Philadelphia to Newtown Square in 1893 which would cross the turnpike at Llanerch. A spur was planned to serve Millbourne Mills, crossing the turnpike just west of 63rd Street, but this section did not open until 1899.

If the Pennsy reached these points first, Shimer knew the giant railroad might be able to permanently block his trolleys from crossing its tracks on the grounds that it would be dangerous. The railroad at Llanerch would be a blind cut and would cross the turnpike at an angle, and the trolley line would be on a hill.

When Pennsylvania Railroad construction crews reached the turnpike at Llanerch in January 1894, they were surprised to find crossing their

Steam dummy No. 4 posed at Broomall in 1895, still in its Frankford and Southwark livery. A small steam boiler powered the front wheels. The cars were a failure, but permitted passenger service to be operated while electrification was completed. Collection of Hilda Shadel Lucas

path a section of double-track about 180 feet long. Shimer also had the forethought to get a temporary injunction preventing the Pennsy from removing his tracks, and he sought a court order to force the railroad to build a grade separation at Llanerch over or under the trolley tracks.

The Pennsy went to court, too, however, and got permission to rip up Shimer's tracks.

Shimer decided to first do battle with the West Philadelphia Passenger Railway, an effort he began just as soon as he got the favorable ruling from the Supreme Court. He wanted to straddle the existing double-track line on Market Street with his own two tracks, and he even hired a contractor for the job. A month later, Shimer presented his construction plans to the Philadelphia Board of Surveyors to get permission to tear up Market Street, but the board refused to issue the permit.

So Shimer, who must have spent a fortune on legal fees, was back in court, this time with a suit seeking to order the board of surveyors to issue the permit. The courts granted the order on December 7, 1894, and the permit was issued later that month.

Then the city of Philadelphia, the West Philadelphia Passenger Railway and a Philadelphia resident each took the matter to court to prevent the turnpike from adding a trolley line to the one which was already operating on Market Street. The case dragged on in the courts for more than two years.

To keep the name of the horsecar line alive during the court fights, the turnpike company re-created the Delaware County Passenger Rail

This conductor's report for January 20, 1896, clearly shows how unsuccessful the steam dummies were. They took an hour and 25 minutes to make the nine-mile trip from 63rd Street to Newtown Square. The other direction required only an hour and 15 minutes because there were fewer hills. For nearly 12 hours of work, this two-man crew produced a total of $1.05 in revenue. PST

Philadelphia & West Chester Traction Company

CONDUCTOR'S REPORT

Run No. _2_ | Engineer _Golding_ | Trips Made _4_

Car No. _10_ | Conductor _Moore_ | " " _4_ | Llanerch, _Jan 20, 1896_

WEST							EAST					
Sixty-third & Market	Leave	6³⁰	9³⁰	12³⁰	3³⁰		Newtown Square	Leave	8⁰⁵	11⁰⁵	2⁰⁵	5⁰⁵
Llanerch	Arrive	6⁵⁰	9⁵⁰	12⁵⁰	3⁵⁰		Water Station	Arrive	8³⁰	11³⁰	2³⁰	5³⁰
	Leave	7⁰⁰	10⁰⁰	1⁰⁰	4⁰⁰			Leave	8³⁵	11³⁵	2³⁵	5³⁵
Water Station	Arrive	7¹⁰	10¹⁰	1¹⁵	4¹⁵		Llanerch	Arrive	8⁵⁰	12⁵⁰	2⁵⁰	5⁵⁰
	Leave	7²⁰	10²⁰	1²⁰	4²⁰			Leave	6⁰⁰	9⁰⁰	12⁰⁰	3⁰⁰
Newtown Square	Arrive	7³⁵	10³⁵	1³⁵	4³⁵		Sixty-third & Market	Arrive	6²⁰	9²⁰	12²⁰	3²⁰

Register No. _561_ Reading, Etc., Start _177_ Finish _204_ Total Fares _27_ Cash $ _1.05_ Passes _6_

1st. East. _6_ West _6_
2nd. do _3_ do _3_
3rd. do _0_ do _4_
4th. do _1_ do _4_

I hereby certify the above to be correct

Wm. Moore .... Conductor

N. B.—Conductor must write on back of this report particulars of anything unusual occuring.

Road Company—although with no stockholders, no president, no treasurer, no board of directors—and appointed Shimer its general manager. It was this company which Shimer planned would actually build the new trolley line.

To further complicate the legal maneuverings, the Philadelphia and West Chester Traction Company was incorporated April 24, 1895. This company was formed under an 1887 law which authorized the creation of new companies to lease, electrify and operate existing railways. But the company could not actually build or own lines.

The plan was that the traction company would lease the railway from the turnpike company, then would acquire control of the turnpike itself by an exchange of stock.

Shimer had the Delaware County Passenger Rail Road enter into a contract on April 1, 1895, with William Wharton, Jr., and Company to construct the trolley line between 63rd Street and Castle Rock, about 10.5 miles.

Trolley cars for the operation were ordered in the name of the turnpike company, but the carbarn and powerhouse equipment were ordered by the Philadelphia, Castle Rock and West Chester Railway. The Wharton Company was supposed to have the entire line finished within 100 working days, barring legal problems.

Difficulties at Llanerch

But Shimer seemed to attract legal problems, and on April 29 another big one occurred when the Pennsy got a temporary injunction against the proposed Llanerch crossing. Shimer went to court again and won permission on May 20 to cross the Pennsy, but only if his line was operated with horse or steam power, just as the original Delaware County Passenger

In August 1895, John Shimer sold to John Sellers 1,310 shares of traction company stock. Shimer continued to own 350 shares. PST

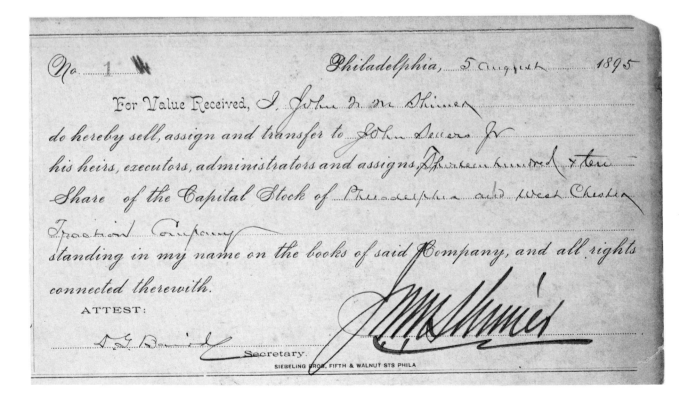

Rail Road charter had called for in the days before electric trolleys had been invented.

Shimer was content with this, because he had a loophole ready. The Pennsy was still not happy and it appealed to the state Supreme Court and got another temporary injunction.

Railroad and trolley construction crews confronted each other at Llanerch, and there were many curses exchanged and occasional fist fights and some threatened shootings.

To make sure the trolley company didn't lay a crossing, the railroad in July stationed a steam engine at the spot. The engine just sat there all day long, right on top of where the crossing should be. Whenever a train came along, the engine naturally had to move for a few minutes. So the railroad put an additional engine there to make sure the crossing would be covered every minute of the day. This time the turnpike company went to court, complaining the locomotives frightened horses on the highway

The traction company's first terminal was at 63rd and Market Streets, at Philadelphia's western boundary. This photograph was taken in 1901, six years before the Market Street Elevated Railway overshadowed the scene. Car No. 7 has just arrived from West Chester. The traction company's combination passenger and baggage station is on the right, and John Sellers' huge Millbourne Mills fills the background. Collection of David H. Cope

and seeking a warrant for the arrest of one of the engineers. When a constable tried to serve the warrant, the engineer threatened to shoot him.

The Supreme Court's injunction finally expired on July 18, and the crossing was then laid. During the often heated Battle of Llanerch Crossing, Shimer had managed to have 11 railroad employees arrested.

The battle would eventually turn out to be a clear-cut victory for the trolley line, because 13 years later—in 1908—the railroad ran its last passenger train to Newtown Square, abandoning service completely due to stiff competition from the trolleys.

At the same time the Pennsy was trying to block the trolley line, seven residents along the route obtained a temporary injunction on April 30, 1895, forbidding Shimer to lay tracks adjacent to their properties, and on May 18 the court issued its decision in the case. The railway, said the judge, could build along the turnpike all the way to Newtown Square under the old horsecar franchise, but it could not build west of Newtown

Square under this franchise. And it also had no right under the franchise to erect poles or overhead trolley wire.

Shimer had apparently anticipated all of this. That was why he had chartered the Philadelphia and West Chester Traction Company. This company would be able to electrify the line after it was built under the Delaware County Passenger Rail Road charter. But the traction company, under law, could not put up the poles and overhead wire until it had obtained the consent of each municipality through which the line passed.

This would be time-consuming, and was one problem Shimer didn't have an answer for.

It didn't remain a problem for long, however, because someone soon suggested buying old steam dummies from the Frankford and Southwark Passenger Railroad Company. The dummies had been replaced by trolley cars and were sitting idle, so Shimer bought nine of them in July 1895, together with a steam-powered snow sweeper, four former horsecar trailers, a turntable and spare parts for a total of $3,000.

Ironically, it was these very same steam dummies which had influenced E. Spencer Miller back in 1864 to seek an amendment to the charter of the horsecar company permitting the use of steam. Even though this amendment hadn't done Miller any good, it proved a godsend for Shimer.

The railway line was formally leased to the traction company on July 18, 1895, and the traction company eventually paid off the $213,547 in construction notes that the Delaware County Passenger Rail Road had issued to the contractors.

At the same time, the traction company acted to acquire ownership of the turnpike. It did so by issuing one share of traction company stock in exchange for two shares of turnpike stock. The transaction was completed by September 1895.

Shimer was delighted when the big day finally arrived on August 15, 1895. After more than 30 years, his boyhood dream of running a railroad out the turnpike was to be fulfilled.

But opening day must have been a sad letdown, for gross receipts totaled a mere 10 cents.

Nobody was pleased with the ugly steam dummies. They were noisy and awkward and clumsy and hot, and they frightened horses and had

The first tickets were issued by the traction company in books of 48 and bore Shimer's signature. PST

The traction company's first electric cars were 15 single-truck summer cars. They were slow and rough riding. PST

The traction company's first six closed cars were four-wheelers. Nos. 5-6 were the first well-built, relatively comfortable cars acquired. They were built by Brill and arrived in 1896. Collection of Andrew W. Maginnis

trouble climbing the hills. A water tower was installed at Darby Creek a mile west of Manoa at the bottom of a small valley. After the dummies stopped to take on water, they often had great difficulty getting up enough momentum to climb the hills.

To be operated properly, dummies were supposed to be turned around at each end of the line. But no turntables or loops were installed on the little railroad, despite the fact that Shimer had acquired one turntable when he bought the dummies. Shimer simply ran the cars backwards in one direction.

Most important, nobody rode the dummies.

They took an hour and 15 minutes to run from 63rd Street to Newtown Square and they were continually off schedule due to breakdowns. Expenses were high and passenger revenues seldom amounted to more than $15 a day. Receipts for the four and a half months of operation during 1895 totaled $1,927 and expenses were an incredible $22,419.

Finally in February 1896, permission had been received from everyone necessary except the Pennsylvania Railroad to string the overhead wire.

Shimer had constructed a small carbarn facing the turnpike just west of the Pennsy crossing in Llanerch, and next to it was the powerhouse. Ironically, Shimer would have to depend completely on the Pennsy to deliver coal to produce his electric power. Conversely, the trolley

Two cars meet at Keystone School switch, three blocks west of Garrett Road, around the turn of the century. Black Horse Hill is in the background, with State Road crossing the tracks halfway up the hill. Wilbur P. Hall

No. 7 crosses the boundary between Delaware and Chester counties near Edgemont on its way to West Chester in 1898. This portion of the West Chester Road west of Newtown Square was not part of the turnpike, and was merely a muddy lane. Collection of Hilda Shadel Lucas

company turned out to be one of the Pennsy's best customers on the Newtown Square branch.

The initial order of cars had been 15 single-truck, 10-bench open summer cars, 30 feet long, built by Lamokin Car Company of Chester, Pennsylvania, and delivered in 1895. They were Nos. 100-114, and had been gathering dust in the carbarn for six months awaiting the end of the legal maneuvering.

With all the overhead wire up except at the Pennsy crossing, Shimer pulled out some of the little electric cars and ran them up and down the line, using a steam dummy to push them across the nonpowered section at Llanerch. But the scheme lasted only one day before Pennsy crews discovered and ripped up the transmission line Shimer had laid under the railroad tracks to provide electric power for the eastern end of the trolley route.

After this, the dummies resumed their chugging between 63rd Street and Llanerch and the electric cars ran the rest of the way to Newtown Square, with passengers transferring at the Pennsy crossing.

This arrangement was a marked improvement over using dummies for the whole distance, but it still left much to be desired. It also subjected passengers to a rather chilly ride during the remainder of the winter on the little open cars.

A Victory for Electricity

So Shimer was back in court again, this time asking to have the injunction removed against stringing trolley wire over the Pennsy. And this time he won. Emphasizing that the proper legal procedures had been followed by leasing the line to the traction company for electrification, the judge dissolved the injunction. But he stipulated that every trolley must stop at the railroad crossing and wait until its conductor got out and signaled that there were no trains coming.

Shimer was elated, and as soon as he got the word he sent two dummies onto the crossing to put up the wire. But the Pennsy hadn't yet heard about the decision, and several railroad men tied ropes around the dummies and yanked them off the tracks with the aid of a steam locomotive.

Ever prepared, Shimer just happened to have a constable standing by who promptly arrested the railroad's roadmaster and a supervisor. That night the railroad men withdrew and the wire finally went up.

The next day—May 6, 1896—the little four-wheel open cars began bobbing along the entire 8.5-mile line, cutting the running time to nearly half of what it had been with the steam dummies.

Six four-wheel closed cars were built or acquired in 1896. Three of them —Nos. 1-3—were rebuilt either from old dummies or from the former horsecars which had been acquired as trailers when the dummies were purchased.

No. 4 was built by Lamokin and was later converted into a freight car. Nos. 5-6, built by Brill, were the first cars lettered with the traction company's name. All the others had been lettered for the turnpike company. The six closed cars and the 15 open cars were all scrapped or sold by 1907 after they had been replaced by bigger and more modern cars.

Trolleys ran between 63rd Street and Newtown Square every 27 minutes, requiring four cars to operate the line. A passenger station was built at 63rd Street.

Shimer's continuing efforts to expand his line eastward into the city were finally dealt a death blow in 1897 when a Philadelphia judge ruled that the Delaware County Passenger Rail Road franchises within Philadelphia were no longer valid, having been surrendered to the city at the same time the portion of the turnpike within the city limits was given up in 1872. Shimer appealed, but the following year the state Supreme Court upheld the lower court ruling.

The financial problems of the trolley line and the turnpike were becoming increasingly more serious. Many turnpike travelers had been scared

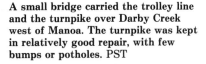

A small bridge carried the trolley line and the turnpike over Darby Creek west of Manoa. The turnpike was kept in relatively good repair, with few bumps or potholes. PST

away by the steam dummies, and now many others were riding the trolleys instead of using the turnpike. Turnpike revenues were down, but not enough people were riding the trolleys to make them break even. Shimer had to borrow money from his partners at L. & R. Wister and Company to pay trolley employees and creditors. He even had to ask for money from the stockholders in the fall of 1897, and money was still owed to the construction company.

The turnpike between Manoa and Darby Creek was almost in ruins, and all profits from 1893 to 1898 were used to buy new stone. With receipts of less than $8,000 a year, it was impossible to properly maintain the road.

Finally the turnpike managers asked the traction company to maintain the highway between Manoa and Newtown Square, but the trolley line was as broke as the turnpike company. In desperation the turnpike

The original powerhouse (left) and carbarn (right) at Llanerch in 1897. West Chester Pike is in the foreground. The shacks in the center functioned as the company's first offices. Next to them is a horse-drawn maintenance wagon, and near the rear of the carbarn is a four-wheel open car with its curtains pulled down. PST

Single-truck cars crowded the interior of the first carbarn. The open car on blocks has probably lent its trucks to a closed car during the winter, a common practice in the early days. This building remained in use until it was torn down in 1971. PST

Wilbur P. Hall, who took many early photographs of the traction company, posed in the Llanerch powerhouse, where he was employed. Collection of Wilbur P. Hall

managers, fearful the courts would throw the road open for free travel because it was so bad, dug into their own pockets to finance the necessary repairs. No dividends were paid during the years Shimer was in control.

Shimer's last major accomplishment was to push through an extension from Newtown Square to West Chester, creating a trolley line 19.75 miles long.

A brochure issued by Shimer to attract new investors claimed that the "railway has been run at a great disadvantage on account of its inability to complete its construction to West Chester. This does not in any way demonstrate the earning power of the completed line, for the town of Newtown Square cannot be considered a profitable terminus. West Chester is a thriving town of 10,000 inhabitants. The population of West Chester demonstrates itself to be a good riding public, as it has 27 westbound trains per day and 26 eastbound trains to Philadelphia."

The running times for the Pennsylvania Railroad trains varied between 70 minutes for express trains and 90 minutes for local trains. The brochure predicted that the trolleys would operate 36 round trips a day. Running time would be 75 minutes to 63rd Street, then another 25 minutes on city trolleys to reach City Hall. "To make this speed, it is necessary to build the road in a substantial manner," said the brochure. "The line will be completely relaid and ballasted," and new cars would be obtained.

Fares on the trolleys from West Chester to 63rd Street would be 25 cents, plus another 5 cents on the city cars. One-way railroad fares were 73 cents for a regular ticket, 58 cents for an excursion ticket, 52 cents for a 10-trip ticket and 23 cents on a monthly ticket.

Since the franchises of the turnpike company and the old horsecar line both ended at Newtown Square, these companies could not build the extension. And neither could the traction company, because it wasn't permitted under law to build anything. It could just electrify, lease and operate.

So the long-dormant Philadelphia, Castle Rock and West Chester Railway was revived. It had a franchise to build as far as Ridley Creek, and a

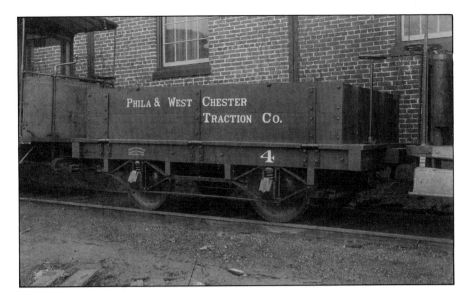

Little four-wheel ballast cars were used in the construction of the West Chester extension in 1898. PST

resolution was passed to extend the line to West Chester. But the Castle Rock company was always really only a paper company, leased to the traction company.

On to West Chester

Shimer once again came through miraculously. The traction company and the turnpike company were both badly in debt, yet he managed to raise $400,000 to build an extension and erase that debt. He did it by making a deal with the construction firm of Pepper and Register. The arrangement would have made the firm the owner of the entire traction company if the company defaulted on its construction payments.

Executed on July 1, 1898, the contract called for the traction company to issue $350,000 in gold bonds and $50,000 in stock to Pepper and Register. The construction firm, in return, would build the extension, provide six new trolleys for it, add a new generator at Llanerch, build a sub-

The Pennsylvania Railroad's subsidiary, the Philadelphia and Delaware County Railroad, opened its line to Newtown Square in 1895. Three daily passenger trains were operated each way until competition from the trolleys finally caused complete abandonment of passenger service in 1908. This schedule is from 1900. PST

PHILADELPHIA & DELAWARE COUNTY RAILROAD.

Distance from Philadel; hia.	STATIONS.	WESTWARD. Week-days.			STATIONS.	EASTWARD. Week-days.		
		85	89	95		86	90	94
		a. m.	p. m.	p. m.		a. m.	p. m.	p. m.
	Philadelphia				Newtown Square	7.22	2.30	5.20
. .	(Broad Street Station).	8.18	3.10	5.49	The Hunt	f 7.27	f 2.35	f 5.25
					Foxcroft	f 7.29	f 2.37	f 5.27
	Leave				Brookthorpe	f 7.32	f 2.40	f 5.30
5.50	Fernwood.	8.35	3.25	6.08	Grassland	7.36	2.44	5.34
6.07	Pembroke	f 8.38	f 3.28	f 6.11	Llanerch	7.40	2.48	5.38
6.77	Wycombe	f 8.40	f 3.30	f 6.13	Arlington	f 7.42	f 2.50	f 5.40
7.26	Garrett Road	f 8.42	f 3.32	f 6.15	Garrett Road	f 7.44	f 2.52	f 5.42
7.97	Arlington	f 8.44	f 3.34	f 6.17	Wycombe	f 7.46	f 2.54	f 5.44
8.92	Llanerch	8.46	3.36	6.19	Pembroke	f 7.48	f 2.56	f 5.46
10.30	Grassland.	8.50	3.40	6.22	Fernwood.	7.52	3.02	5.50
11.80	Brookthorpe	f 8.54	f 3.44	f 6.25	Arrive			
12.68	Foxcroft	f 8.56	f 3.46	f 6.27				
13.37	The Hunt	f 8.58	f 3.48	f 6.30	Philadelphia			
15.37	Newtown Square	9.03	3.53	6.35	(Broad Street Station).	8.12	3.20	6.05
		a. m.	p. m.	p. m.		a. m.	p. m.	p. m.

"f" Stops only on notice to Agent or Conductor, or on signal.

station at Ridley Creek, reballast the line east of Newtown Square and pay off the existing debts of the traction company and the turnpike company.

Pepper and Register set up temporary headquarters at Castle Rock, near where Shimer grew up, and used the extensive rock there for ballasting the extension. Work began at Newtown Square and moved westward, bypassing sections where the permission of adjacent landowners had not yet been secured.

By the end of November the track had been built as far as the West Chester borough limits.

Borough council wanted the trolleys to enter the town on Market Street, then use Adams Street to reach Gay Street. Shimer wanted to go straight down Gay Street to Adams Street, and council finally agreed. Gay Street is an extension of West Chester Pike and is the town's main business street.

When it reached West Chester, the trolley line simply moved from the south side of the road into the center of Gay Street to reach the end of the line.

The first trolleys ran to the terminus at Gay and Adams Streets on December 17, 1898, amidst a huge celebration. The first car was filled with officials, who had a leisurely dinner at a nearby hotel while residents examined their first trolley car from Philadelphia.

When Shimer chartered the Philadelphia, Castle Rock and West Chester back in 1892, the *West Chester Daily Local* had proclaimed: "Let it come. Trolley from the East, thou art welcome." Now it was here, but

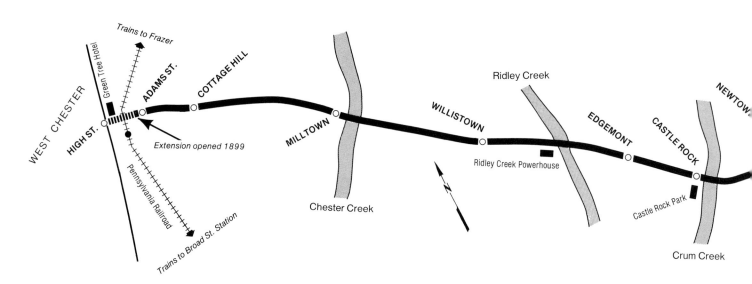

West Chester Line, 1898

the official opening two weeks later was a fiasco.

Fighting their way through heavy snow over only partially ballasted roadbed on December 31, 1898, it took the two new trolley cars filled with officials more than four hours to reach Gay and Adams Streets. A banquet at the Green Tree Hotel followed a brief celebration, then the officials prepared to head back to Philadelphia.

But the lead car jumped the track near Milltown—presumably because of the snow—and everybody had to go back to West Chester and board a Pennsylvania Railroad train for Philadelphia.

Regular service was supposed to begin on December 31, but the snow delayed it until January 4, 1899. Even then service was sporadic because the line was still being finished and ballast cars were continually getting in the way of regular passenger cars.

The six new double-truck cars provided by Pepper and Register—Nos. 7-12—arrived in late 1898 and remained in service until 1912. Built by Jackson and Sharp Company, the six cars seated 40 passengers and contained a separate smoking compartment. They were painted dark red with gold striping and lettering and cost $4,700 each. They were the first double-truck cars on the line, and were much more comfortable and reliable than the older cars.

Dark red remained the primary color for all of the company's passenger cars for the next three-quarters of a century.

Although Shimer had seemingly done a superb job, he had left the traction company and the turnpike company in extremely poor financial condition and had probably created many enemies.

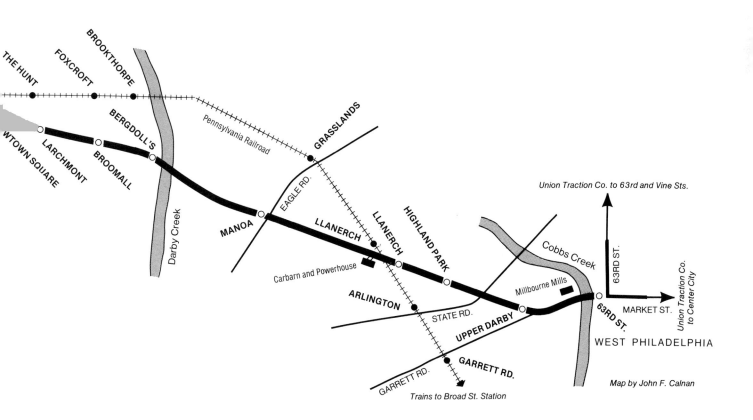

Nos. 7-12 were the first double-truck cars, acquired when the West Chester extension opened in 1898. They included separate smoking compartments and were much more comfortable and reliable than the single-truck cars. Collection of Fred W. Schneider, III

The interiors of Nos. 7-12 were spartan, with wood slat floors and rattan seats. Collection of Fred W. Schneider, III

View of the motorman's position of Nos. 7-12. Passengers entered and left by the rear door, where the conductor was stationed. Wilbur P. Hall

Sadly enough, the same month the line to West Chester opened turned out to be the last month Shimer would ever exert any influence over the affairs of the trolley company. That month he was defeated by an outsider who replaced him as president of the company. Shimer remained a director of the traction company for several more years, but never again did he exert any influence over its management.

His name quickly faded into history, perpetuated only by "Shimer's Siding," a passing track east of Broomall.

A sign at Toll Gate No. 4 in Manoa advised travelers: "Stop. Give ticket or pay toll." The turnpike narrowed to a single lane in front of the toll house to make it more difficult for turnpike users to sneak by without paying their tolls. PST

A branch of the Pennsylvania Railroad's Newtown Square line was built
to Millbourne Mills in 1899. It was
later extended to 69th Street Terminal.
The traction company's 63rd Street
Terminal was just out of the picture to
the left. Collection of Hilda Shadel
Lucas

Chapter 3

Taylor Expands the System, 1899-1913

THE CONSTRUCTION FIRM OF PEPPER AND REGISTER had been paid principally in traction company bonds for its work in extending the trolley line from Newtown Square to West Chester.

In June 1898, even before the contract with the traction company was signed, David Pepper, president of the company, contacted the prominent Philadelphia law firm of Page, Allison and Penrose to seek assistance in selling the bonds. A young man named A. Merritt Taylor had just been named head of the law firm's real estate and investment counseling department, and to him fell the job of unloading the $1,000 bonds at $850 each. This was Taylor's first connection with the traction company, and he was only 24 years old at the time.

Taylor had quit school when he was 15 to work in the machine shop of William Sellers and Company. He had been born to Quaker parents in Burlington, New Jersey, on March 2, 1874, and he attended Penn Charter School in Philadelphia and Westtown Boarding School a few miles east of West Chester. Both schools were operated by the Quakers.

After four years as an apprentice and a machinist, Taylor ventured into the investment securities business. Nothing in his background, however, gave him any expertise in electric railway matters.

But Taylor was an ambitious young man on the way up, and he immediately became interested in the Philadelphia and West Chester Traction Company after getting the job of selling the Pepper and Register bonds. Here was a struggling little country trolley line with a potentially fabulous future, just the sort of thing that could further his career if he handled it properly.

The more he thought about it, the more interested he became.

He spent much time riding the uncomfortable little four-wheel cars back and forth between 63rd Street and Newtown Square that summer, looking over the property and coming up with ideas for improving and expanding it. The biggest idea in the back of his mind was a high-speed connection between the traction company's cars and Center City Philadelphia.

The only connection then was on slow streetcars that ran 63 blocks all the way down crowded Market Street. New York City had been building elevated railroads over its congested streets since 1871, and Boston had just finished the first subway in America. Already there was talk of this sort of thing for Philadelphia, and it was inevitable that elevated lines and subways had to come someday soon. And what more logical place could there be to build them than on Market Street, the city's main thoroughfare?

Taylor decided he wanted to be a part of all this when it happened.

A. Merritt Taylor, who became president of the traction company in 1899. Photograph was taken in 1913. PST

Special tickets for use by Pepper and Register employees during completion of the West Chester extension in 1899. PST

He had several long talks that summer with John Sellers, Jr., and managed to convince the old man to support him in his bid to wrest control of the traction company from John Shimer. The Sellers family still owned a major block of the stock, and the backing of family head John Sellers would be necessary to accomplish anything.

Though Shimer had done an extraordinary job considering his meager resources, he had left both the traction company and the turnpike company in very poor financial condition. The trolley line was also in poor physical condition, and was not attracting enough riders to earn a profit.

By 1898, Sellers and some of the other major stockholders were rapidly becoming disenchanted by the lack of dividends and the bleak-looking financial future.

Sellers must have lost faith in Shimer and must have had a great deal of confidence in this brash young man who was plotting openly to take over the company.

Taylor bought his first five shares of stock on September 1, 1898, chiefly so he could qualify to become a member of the board of directors. Sellers managed to get him on the board later that month.

Taylor asked Pepper and Register to pay him partly in stock for selling their bonds, and on September 20 he got 50 shares. He received another 127 shares from Pepper and Register on December 9, and during January he rapidly bought up as much as he could. By mid-January 1899, when it was time for the annual election of officers, he owned 690 of the 7,160 shares outstanding—nearly one-tenth of all the stock.

Shimer owned 443 shares and three relatives owned 24 more.

Sensing he was in for a fight, Shimer made his annual report to the stockholders as optimistic as possible. He spoke of the "well-ballasted railway" (although it wasn't at that time) and of the "magnificent, broad highway" owned by the company (which was again in miserable disrepair).

"Your company has materially prospered during the past 12 months," Shimer wrote in his annual report. "Your receipts have been larger, and your operating expenses have been materially reduced. . . . Everything has been done in the most substantial manner, with the best material, and it is hoped that your gross receipts [for 1899] will be multiplied by three, as your operating expenses will not be increased more than one-half what they now are. . . ."

Shimer apologized for the irregular schedules being maintained on the West Chester line, saying he hoped the line "will be in full working order by spring, although the ballasting may not be entirely finished until the early summer."

"No small amount of praise is due your board of directors for the untiring efforts they have exerted in your company's behalf," he told the stockholders.

Despite his glowing report, Shimer lost the election on January 13, 1899. Taylor voted for himself and convinced two of the other directors to side with him. Shimer voted for himself, but got the support of only one other director.

Overly confident that he could put the rundown and poorly patronized line in top condition within a very short time, Taylor agreed to serve as president without pay until the company started paying dividends. Meanwhile, he remained associated with Page, Allison and Penrose. But Taylor soon realized he had committed himself to more than he had anticipated.

The new Llanerch office and waiting room built in 1899. The powerhouse is on the left, and a single-truck closed car peeks out of the carbarn on the right. PST

The new building served as the dispatcher's office, and all conductors and motormen began and ended their day here. PST

A bowling alley was built in the basement of the Llanerch office building for the use of employees. In a special ceremony, A. Merritt Taylor (left) challenged Connie Mack, owner of the Philadelphia Athletics baseball team. There is no record of who won. PST

"When I was elected president I naturally expected to find the books of the company in good condition and all of the machinery and equipments in good repair. As a matter of fact I found that the books were very inaccurate and misleading." And he found the physical plant in poor condition.

By June, he began to realize he had a mammoth task ahead of him, and he asked to be put on the payroll, a request which was quickly granted. His salary was $4,000 a year.

The year ending June 30, 1899, produced a deficit of $12,412. Realizing that it was going to take much longer than he had originally thought before the profits would start pouring in, Taylor took steps to ensure that he would not be ousted as president before he had finished rebuilding the company.

In May 1899, he asked the largest stockholders to agree not to dispose of their holdings to outsiders for at least two years. Most of the shareholders signed the agreement, but Shimer and his friends refused to.

The extension to West Chester was only partially ballasted when Taylor took over the company and the trolleys were still running irregularly because work cars kept getting in their way on the single-track line.

The first major accident occurred on March 22, 1899, on the uncompleted line at the West Chester borough limits. A passenger car motored by David P. Ortlip passed the only other passenger car on the line near Milltown on a dark, foggy night. It had been raining, and Ortlip and his conductor, Elwood Thompson, had just come on duty.

Ortlip and Thompson claimed they got a clear signal at Race Track Siding, which meant there should have been no other cars between there and the end of the line at Adams Street. Traffic was light, and Ortlip was running rapidly when suddenly at 8:05 p.m. his car smashed into a ballast car hauled by one of the small open cars.

No. 12 passes the new water tower erected at Llanerch to supply the traction company's sprinkler car. PST

Ortlip lost a leg and was given a job as a toll collector. He also filed a suit against the traction company—which he won—charging negligence.

The Llanerch station of the Pennsylvania Railroad was directly across West Chester Pike from the traction company's office building. The railroad had a passenger agent and a freight agent on duty at Llanerch. PST

A Newtown Square-bound train is crossing West Chester Pike in 1900. The railroad station is on the left, and the traction company has constructed a second carbarn on the right. PST

Track Troubles

The accident, however, was only a small part of Taylor's troubles during those early months of 1899. The track on the new extension was in such an unfinished state that it was nearly impossible to maintain the schedules west of Newtown Square. Four cars operated a 25-minute frequency between 63rd Street and Newtown Square from January 8 to May 10. Then passengers had to change to two small cars which were trying to run every 50 minutes between Newtown Square and West Chester.

In the extremely hilly area between Newtown Square and Milltown, the little cars kept jumping the track. One passenger broke two ribs during a derailment, and she sued the company. The rails on the steep hills had a tendency to creep downward on hot days. At the bottom of the hills, the rails would buckle outward, and one motorman described the track as often looking like a snake.

Taylor didn't know what to do. He posted track gangs at frequent intervals along the line to watch for the buckling and to warn motormen. But still the cars kept falling off the track.

"We were at our wits' end to know what to do to stop the cars from jumping the track and delaying the schedule," Taylor testified three years later during a court case in which the traction company was sued by Pepper and Register for refusing to pay for the shoddy construction work.

Finally, J.W. Silliman, the traction company's chief engineer, invented and installed "anti-creeping devices" on the hills and the problem was solved—but at great expense.

At the same time the buckling was occurring, there were serious power shortages west of Milltown.

"I traveled back and forth on the road on an average of three or four days per week, and upon each trip I noticed that for some reason the cars ran very slowly uphill and at times could not run up certain hills at a speed of over two miles an hour; they simply dragged along," Taylor testified. "I also noticed when riding in the cars in the evening the electric lights would become so dim that it became impossible for me to read a paper. The wire in the lamps became merely a red-hot wire, giving out practically no illumination."

In addition to all that, the current occasionally went off on the western portion of the line, sometimes for as long as half an hour.

The low voltage was burning up the motors of the trolleys at a tremendous rate.

Silliman suggested running feed wires from the Ridley Creek Substation to other parts of the line, and after installing much feed wire and

Interior of the Llanerch powerhouse in 1899. PST

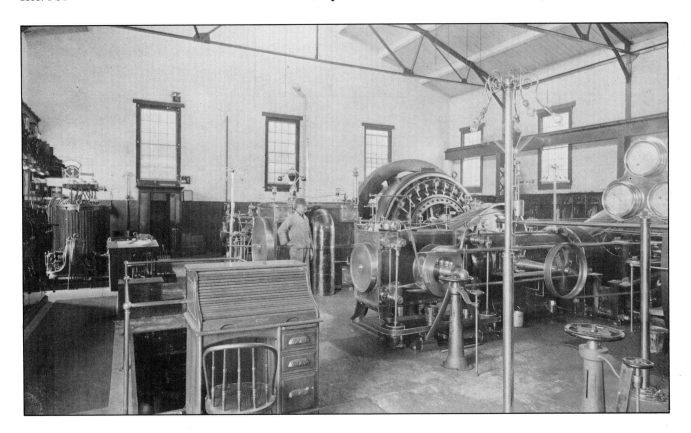

The sprinkler car obtained by Taylor in 1899 was used to wet down the highway to control dust in the summer months. The primitive-looking car remained in service until the turnpike was paved. Wilbur P. Hall

some additional equipment in the substation the cars ran reasonably well.

On May 10, Taylor tried running all cars directly through to West Chester from 63rd Street in an hour and 25 minutes. But on June 12 he was forced to lengthen the schedule by 10 minutes. When all the feed wire was up, the cars again started running every half hour beginning August 10 on an hour and 25 minute running time.

Another problem was that the switches had been built so sharp by Pepper and Register that passengers were thrown out of their seats unless the cars went very slow, and the flanges of the car wheels bumped into the tongues of the switches, breaking off parts of the flanges and ultimately requiring new wheels.

The company's headquarters building was a mere shack next to the little carbarn at Llanerch, and the area was cluttered with the remains of old steam dummies and other junk when Taylor took over. The trolleys had been poorly maintained due to lack of funds, and the boiler tubes in the Llanerch powerhouse had seldom been cleaned out and were badly clogged.

Worst of all, Shimer had neglected to obtain any snow-fighting equipment. So when a blizzard descended on the trolley line a month after he had taken over, Taylor hired 175 men for a week to dig out his railway.

Sprucing Things Up

While Pepper and Register were slowly completing work on the line to Gay and Adams Streets, Taylor hired another contractor to extend the track a third of a mile further on to Gay and High Streets. The new terminus was in the downtown business district and in front of the locally famous Green Tree Inn, where sumptuous full-course dinners cost 50 cents. Regular service began to High Street on June 1, with trolleys departing from West Chester every half hour. Sometimes on Saturdays and Sundays there were so many people that the cars ran every 15 minutes as thousands rode just to take a look at the new line.

An additional car—No. 13—arrived from Jackson and Sharp. It was nearly identical to Nos. 7-12.

Within a year Taylor had torn down the shack which had served as the Llanerch office and constructed a new stone office building with a well-manicured lawn surrounding it. The steam dummies were sold, the carbarn was doubled in size and the whole property was cleaned up.

Several of the four-wheel open cars were sold and five double-truck open cars—Nos. 101-105—were purchased in 1900 to provide a speedier and more comfortable ride. The big open cars were used only during warm weather, and as they sped up and down the hills to West Chester passengers said it felt like riding a roller coaster. The arrival of No. 13 and the new open cars meant that none of the single-truck cars had to be used in regular service, which improved service reliability and speed.

Any doubts John Sellers and the other directors may have had about Taylor's abilities when they voted him into office were quickly dispelled. Taylor turned out to be an absolute dynamo. He took over a system in January 1899 that was basically a cheaply built, poorly patronized, run-down country trolley line. By the following year he had literally accomplished miracles. He obtained new passenger cars and new work equipment, extended the line in West Chester, improved the reliability and frequency of service, improved the power supply, doubled the size of the carbarn, built new company offices, disposed of derelict cars, obtained new insurance policies, obtained additional revenue from advertising on

Taylor issued a new timetable a month after he took over as president. Trolleys left 63rd Street every 25 minutes on weekdays, with alternate cars running all the way to West Chester. Chester County Historical Society

ATTRACTIONS

BEAUTIFUL VIEWS

ROCK BALLAST ROAD
FROM PHILADELPHIA
TO WEST CHESTER

NO DUST—NO CINDERS

MAGNIFICENT EQUIPMENT

New combination cars such as have never been in the vicinity of Philadelphia. They contain spacious smoking compartments and are arranged with all seats facing the front with an isle down the centre. The heat and light are both supplied by electricity and the cars are equipped with air brakes, which add much to the comfort of passengers.

Castle Rock Park, a most interesting spot, is owned by the Company, and passengers will be well repaid by stopping off there, as the curious formation of the rocks has, in the past, attracted sight-seers from long distances. This Park will be open as a picnic ground for the patrons of the road during the coming Summer, and every facility will be given schools and other organizations which wish to avail themselves of this beautiful spot for picnic parties.

Special Cars May Be Chartered

For any further information address the office of the Company.

726 Drexel Building, Philadelphia

TIME TABLE

February 24, 1899

Philadelphia

and

West Chester

Traction Co.

A. MERRITT TAYLOR
President

the cars, built a waiting room at Llanerch, installed line phones for better communication and public phones for the convenience of passengers, built houses at Llanerch for maintenance employees so they would be on call for emergencies, repainted the older cars, improved trackwork and ballasting, rebuilt many track switches, constructed a freight station at 63rd Street for use by the milk trolley, reduced the price of tickets bought in bulk (200 for $9), opened an amusement park at Castle Rock, installed new boilers, engines and generators at the Llanerch powerhouse, built three small passenger stations along the line and greatly improved the morale of the company's employees.

The same year he became president, Taylor also ordered two snow-plows, a snow sweeper, a new and bigger milk car to handle the increasing business and a sprinkler car. The sprinkler replaced horse-drawn wagons which wet down the dusty highway in the summer in an effort to prevent patrons of both the toll road and the trolley line from choking to death. The trucks of the sprinkler car were used in the winter on one of the snowplows.

At the same time, he was planning extensions to his trolley line, and in the summer of 1899 he took over the nation's oldest turnpike company, the Philadelphia and Lancaster Turnpike Road Company.

Taylor wanted to extend his line westward from West Chester to Coatesville, about 13 miles. For a few miles north of West Chester the line would be on private right-of-way, then it would run next to the Philadel-

WESTBOUND—WEEKDAYS				EASTBOUND—WEEKDAYS			
Leave 63d & Market Sts. Phila	Llanerch	Newtown Square	Arrive West Chester	Leave West Chester	Newtown Square	Llanerch	Arrive 63d & Market Sts. Phila
. . . .	. . . .	. . . .	. . . .	. . . .	. . . .	5.15 AM	5.31 AM
. . . .	. . . .	. . . .	. . . .	. . . .	. . . .	5.40 "	5.56 "
. . . .	. . . .	. . . .	. . . .	. . . .	. . . .	6.05 "	6.21 "
. . . .	5.28 AM	6.02 AM	6.50 AM	. . . .	6.02 AM	6.30 "	6.46 "
5.34 AM	5.53 "	6 27 "	. . . .	. . . .	6.27 "	6.55 "	7.11 "
5.59 "	6.18 "	6.52 "	7.40 "	. . . .	6.52 "	7.20 "	7.36 "
6.24 "	6.43 "	7.17 "	. . . .	. . . .	7.17 "	7.45 "	8.01 "
6.49 "	7 08 "	7.42 "	8.30 "	7.00 AM	7.42 "	8.10 "	8.26 "
7.14 "	7.33 "	8.07 "	. . . .	. . . .	8.07 "	8.35 "	8.51 "
7.39 "	7.58 "	8.32 "	9.20 "	7.50 "	8.32 "	9.00 "	9.16 "
8.04 "	8.23 "	8.57 "	. . . .	. . . .	8 57 "	9.25 "	9.41 "
8.29 "	8.48 "	9.22 "	10.10 "	8 40 "	9.22 "	9.50 "	10.06 "
8.54 "	9.13 "	9.47 "	. . . .	. . . .	9.47 "	10.15 "	10.31 "
9.19 "	9.38 "	10.12 "	11.00 "	9.30 "	10.12 "	10.40 "	10.56 "
9.44 "	10.03 "	10.37 "	. . . .	. . . .	10.37 "	11.05 "	11.21 "
10.09 "	10.28 "	11.02 "	11.50 "	10.20 "	11.02 "	11.30 "	11.46 "
10 34 "	10.53 "	11.27 "	. . . .	. . . .	11.27 "	11.55 "	12.11 PM
10.59 "	11.18 "	11.52 "	12.40 PM	11.10 "	11.52 "	12.20 PM	12.36 "
11.24 "	11.43 "	12.17 PM	. . . .	. . . .	12.17 PM	12 45 "	1.01 "
11.49 "	12.08 PM	12.42 "	1.30 "	12.00 N'N	12.42 "	1.10 "	1.26 "
12.14 PM	12.33 "	1.07 "	. . . .	. . . .	1.07 "	1.35 "	1.51 "
12.39 "	12.58 "	1.32 "	2.20 "	12.50 PM	1.32 "	2.00 "	2.16 "
1.04 "	1.23 "	1.57 "	. . . .	. . . .	1.57 "	2.25 "	2.41 "
1.29 "	1.48 "	2.22 "	3.10 "	1.40 "	2.22 "	2.50 "	3.06 "
1.54 "	2.13 "	2.47 "	. . . .	. . . .	2.47 "	3.15 "	3.31 "
2.19 "	2.38 "	3.12 "	4.00 "	2 30 "	3.12 "	3.40 "	3.56 "
2.44 "	3.03 "	3.37 "	. . . .	. . . .	3.37 "	4.05 "	4.21 "
3.09 "	3.28 "	4.02 "	4.50 "	3.20 "	4.02 "	4.30 "	4.46 "
3.34 "	3.53 "	4.27 "	. . . .	. . . .	4 27 "	4.55 "	5.11 "
3.59 "	4.18 "	4.52 "	5.40 "	4.10 "	4.52 "	5.20 "	5.36 "
4.24 "	4.43 "	5.17 "	. . . .	. . . .	5.17 "	5.45 "	6.01 "
4 49 "	5.08 "	5.42 "	6.30 "	5.00 "	5.42 "	6.10 "	6.26 "
5.14 "	5.33 "	6.07 "	. . . .	. . . .	6.07 "	6.35 "	6.51 "
5.39 "	5.58 "	6 32 "	7.20 "	5.50 "	6.32 "	7.00 "	7.16 "
6.04 "	6.23 "	6.57 "	. . . .	. . . .	6.57 "	7.25 "	7.41 "
6.29 "	6.48 "	7.22 "	8.10 "	6.40 "	7.22 "	7.50 "	8.06 "
6.54 "	7 13 "	7.47 "	. . . .	. . . .	7.47 "	8.15 "	8.31 "
7.19 "	7.38 "	8.12 "	9.00 "	7.30 "	8.12 "	8.40 "	8.56 "
7.44 "	8 03 "	8.37 "	. . . .	. . . .	8.37 "	9.05 "	9.21 "
8.09 "	8.28 "	9.02 "	9.50 "	8.20 "	9.02 "	9.30 "	9.46 "
8.34 "	8.53 "	9.27 "	. . . .	. . . .	9.27 "	9.55 "	10.11 "
8 59 "	9.18 "	9.52 "	10.40 "	9.10 "	9.52 "	10.20 "	10.36 "
9 24 "	9 43 "	10.17 "	. . . .	. . . .	10.17 "	10.45 "	11.01 "
9.49 "	10.08 "	10.42 "	. . . .	10.00 "	10.42 "	11.10 "	11.26 "
10 14 "	10.33 "	11 07 "	. . . .	. . . .	11.07 "	11.35 "	11.51 "
10.39 "	10.58 "	11.32 "	. . . .	10.50 "	11.32 "	12.00 N'T	12.16 AM
11.04 "	11 23 "	11 57 "	. . . .	. . . .	11.57 "	12.24 AM	. . . .
11.29 "	11.48 "	. . . .	. . . .	12.47 AM	1.14 "	. . . .	. . . .
11.54 "	12.13 AM	12.47 AM	. . . .				
12.19 AM	12.37 "	. . . .	. . . .				

WESTBOUND—SUNDAYS				EASTBOUND—SUNDAYS			
Leave 63d & Market Sts. Phila	Llanerch	Newtown Square	Arrive West Chester	Leave West Chester	Newtown Square	Llanerch	Arrive 63d & Market Sts. Phila
. . . .	. . . .	. . . .	. . . .	. . . .	. . . .	5.45 AM	5.59 AM
. . . .	. . . .	. . . .	. . . .	. . . .	. . . .	6.15 "	6.29 "
. . . .	. . . .	. . . .	. . . .	. . . .	. . . .	6.45 "	6.59 "
6.00 AM	6.15 AM	6.46 AM	7.25 AM	. . . .	6.46 "	7.15 "	7.29 "
6.30 "	6.45 "	7.16 "	7.55 "	. . . .	7.16 "	7.45 "	7.59 "
7.00 "	7.15 "	7.46 "	8.25 "	. . . .	7.46 "	8.15 "	8.29 "
7.30 "	7.45 "	8.16 "	8.55 "	7.30 AM	8.16 "	8.45 "	8.59 "
8.00 "	8.15 "	8.46 "	9.25 "	8.00 "	8.46 "	9.15 "	9.29 "
8.30 "	8.45 "	9.16 "	9.55 "	8.30 "	9.16 "	9.45 "	9.59 "
9.00 "	9.15 "	9.46 "	10.25 "	9.00 "	9.46 "	10.15 "	10.29 "
9.30 "	9.45 "	10.16 "	10.55 "	9.30 "	10.16 "	10.45 "	10.59 "
10.00 "	10.15 "	10.46 "	11.25 "	10.00 "	10.46 "	11.15 "	11.29 "
10.30 "	10.45 "	11.16 "	11.55 "	10.30 "	11.16 "	11.45 "	11.59 "
11.00 "	11.15 "	11.46 "	12.25 PM	11.00 "	11.46 "	12.15 PM	12.29 PM
11.30 "	11.45 "	12.16 PM	12.55 "	11.30 "	12.16 PM	12.45 "	12.59 "
12.00 N'N	12.15 PM	12.46 "	1.25 "	12.00 N'N	12.46 "	1.15 "	1.29 "
12.30 PM	12.45 "	1.16 "	1.55 "	12.30 PM	1.16 "	1.45 "	1.59 "
1.00 "	1.15 "	1.46 "	2.25 "	1.00 "	1.46 "	2.15 "	2.29 "
1.30 "	1.45 "	2.16 "	2.55 "	1.30 "	2.16 "	2.45 "	2.59 "
2.00 "	2.15 "	2.46 "	3.25 "	2.00 "	2.46 "	3.15 "	3.29 "
2.30 "	2.45 "	3.16 "	3 55 "	2.30 "	3.16 "	3.45 "	3.59 "
3.00 "	3.15 "	3.46 "	4.25 "	3.00 "	3.46 "	4.15 "	4.29 "
3.30 "	3.45 "	4.16 "	4.55 "	3.30 "	4.16 "	4.45 "	4.59 "
4.00 "	4.15 "	4.46 "	5.25 "	4.00 "	4.46 "	5.15 "	5.29 "
4.30 "	4.45 "	5.16 "	5.55 "	4.30 "	5.16 "	5.45 "	5.59 "
5.00 "	5.15 "	5.46 "	6.25 "	5.00 "	5.46 "	6.15 "	6.29 "
5.30 "	5.45 "	6.16 "	6.55 "	5.30 "	6.16 "	6.45 "	6.59 "
6.00 "	6.15 "	6.46 "	7.25 "	6.00 "	6.46 "	7.15 "	7.29 "
6.30 "	6.45 "	7.16 "	7.55 "	6.30 "	7.16 "	7.45 "	7.59 "
7 00 "	7.15 "	7.46 "	8.25 "	7.00 "	7.46 "	8.15 "	8.29 "
7.30 "	7.45 "	8.16 "	8.55 "	7.30 "	8.16 "	8.45 "	8.59 "
8.00 "	8.15 "	8.46 "	9.25 "	8.00 "	8.46 "	9.15 "	9.29 "
8.30 "	8.45 "	9.16 "	9.55 "	8.30 "	9.16 "	9.45 "	9.59 "
9.00 "	9.15 "	9.46 "	10.25 "	9.00 "	9.46 "	10.15 "	10.29 "
9.30 "	9.45 "	10.16 "	10.55 "	9.30 "	10.16 "	10.45 "	10.59 "
10.00 "	10.15 "	10.46 "	11.25 "	10.00 "	10.46 "	11.15 "	11.29 "
10.30 "	10.45 "	11.16 "	. . . .	10.30 "	11.16 "	11.45 "	11.59 "
11.00 "	11.15 "	11.46 "	. . . .	11.00 "	11.46 "	12.15 AM	12.29 AM
11.30 "	11.45 "	12.16 AM	. . . .	11.30 "	12.16 AM	12.45 "	. . . .
12.00 N'T	12.15 AM	. . . .	. . . .				
12.30 AM	12.45 "	. . . .	. . . .				

NOTE.—This time table is temporary and subject to change without notice. The number and speed of cars will be greatly increased as soon as the ballasting of the road is completed. The line is divided into five sections between Philadelphia and West Chester, upon each of which sections a fare of 5 cents is collected, making the total fare from Philadelphia to West Chester 25 cents. The distance is 19½ miles.

phia and Lancaster Turnpike the rest of the way to Coatesville. Just to make sure he wouldn't have any trouble getting permission from the managers of the Lancaster turnpike to run his trolleys along their road, Taylor arranged to purchase the entire turnpike company.

This had been the first turnpike company in the country when it was chartered in 1792. Construction of a 65-mile plank road had been completed in 1796 at a cost of $465,000. The first stage coaches on the new road made the trip between Philadelphia and Lancaster in 12 hours. But a railroad was built right next to the turnpike in 1836 and steam locomotives began hauling freight and passengers much faster than they could move along the old plank road. By 1899 the Lancaster company had sold all of its toll road east of Paoli and west of Coatesville.

Taylor had the traction company purchase 1,034 of the 1,155 shares of outstanding stock in the Philadelphia and Lancaster company during the summer of 1899. Then he had himself named as trustee of the company.

Below:

Taylor constructed a short extension of the West Chester line from Gay and Adams Streets to Gay and High Streets in 1899. The extension brought the traction company's cars into the center of West Chester's business district. The Green Tree Inn is on the left in this 1899 view. PST

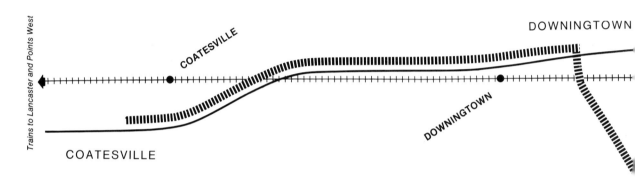

Taylor's Proposed Extensions, 1900

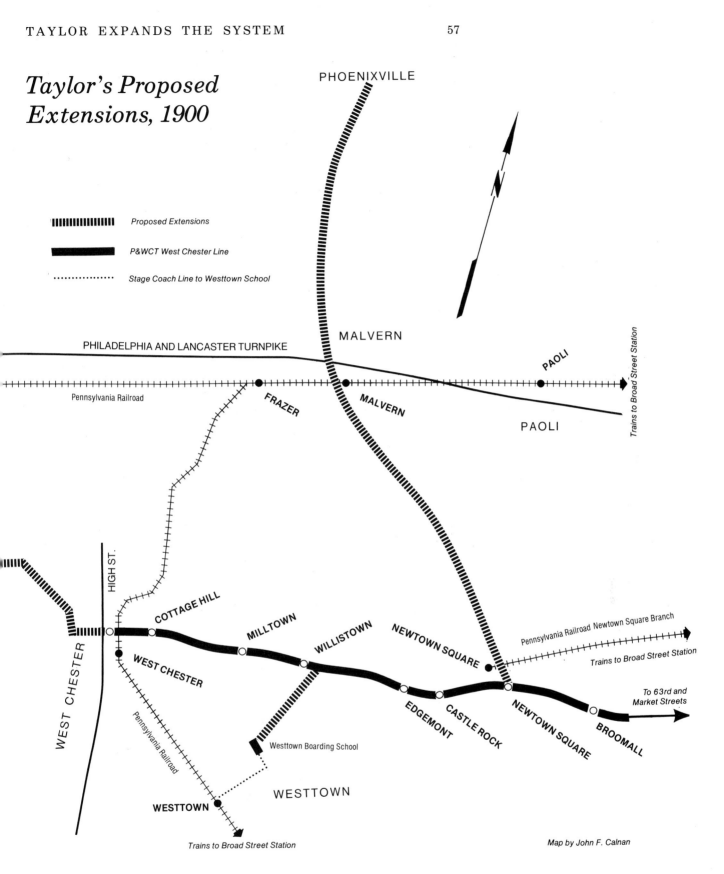

|||||||||||||||||||	*Proposed Extensions*
▬▬▬▬▬▬▬	*P&WCT West Chester Line*
··············	*Stage Coach Line to Westtown School*

PHOENIXVILLE

PHILADELPHIA AND LANCASTER TURNPIKE

MALVERN

PAOLI

Trains to Broad Street Station

Pennsylvania Railroad

FRAZER

MALVERN

PAOLI

HIGH ST.

COTTAGE HILL

MILLTOWN

WILLISTOWN

NEWTOWN SQUARE

Pennsylvania Railroad Newtown Square Branch

Trains to Broad Street Station

WEST CHESTER

WEST CHESTER

EDGEMONT

CASTLE ROCK

NEWTOWN SQUARE

BROOMALL

To 63rd and Market Streets

Pennsylvania Railroad

Westtown Boarding School

WESTTOWN

WESTTOWN

Trains to Broad Street Station

Map by John F. Calnan

At a reorganization meeting the following January 8, Taylor elected himself president. He had the company's board of managers pass a resolution on February 14, 1900, to permit the Philadelphia, Castle Rock and West Chester Railway Company to "construct, maintain and operate a double or single-track railway" along a portion of the turnpike.

Extension Is Thwarted

He asked the boroughs of West Chester and Downingtown and the city of Coatesville to pass ordinances permitting the trolley line to run on certain streets, and everything appeared to be going well. But the proposed trolley line would have paralleled the big Pennsylvania Railroad. Indeed, it would have run right next to it for several miles. The Pennsy had lost the Battle of Llanerch Crossing four years earlier, and it did not intend to lose this encounter with the traction company's new president.

The railroad made certain that it and one of its employees owned some of the land that Taylor's proposed line would have to cross to reach the Lancaster turnpike. Naturally, they refused to permit the trolley to cross their land, and at that time there was no right of eminent domain for electric railway companies. So Taylor gave up the whole plan and turned his attention to other extensions.

The traction company did not end up owning the Lancaster turnpike for very long, because in 1901 the road was condemned and turned over

A joint timetable was issued showing service from Philadelphia to Lancaster via trolleys of the traction company, the West Chester Street Railway and Conestoga Traction Company. The trip required four hours and 15 minutes. PST

PHILADELPHIA, 69th Street, to WEST CHESTER, DOWNINGTOWN, COATESVILLE, LANCASTER and intermediate Towns.

PHILA. 69th STREET	WEST CHESTER Arr.	WEST CHESTER Lv.	DOWN-ING-TOWN.	COATESVILLE Arr.	COATESVILLE Lv.	LAN-CASTER
		5 40	6 12	6 37	6 45	8 45
5 32	6 42	6 50	7 24	7 48	7 50	9 45
6 32	7 42	7 50	8 24	8 48	8 50	10 45
7 30	8 42	8 50	9 24	9 48	9 50	11 45
8 30	9 42	9 50	10 24	10 48	10 50	12 45
9 30	10 42	10 50	11 24	11 48	11 50	1 45
10 30	11 42	11 50	12 24	12 48	12 50	2 45
11 30	12 42	12 50	1 24	1 48	1 50	3 45
12 30	1 42	1 50	2 24	2 48	2 50	4 45
1 30	2 42	2 50	3 24	3 48	3 50	5 45
2 30	3 42	3 50	4 24	4 48	4 50	6 45
3 30	4 42	4 50	5 24	5 48	5 50	7 45
4 30	5 42	5 50	6 24	6 48	6 50	8 45
5 30	6 42	6 50	7 24	7 48	7 50	9 45
6 30	7 42	7 50	8 24	8 48	8 50	10 45
7 30	8 42	8 50	9 24	9 48	9 50	11 45
8 30	9 42	9 50	10 24	10 48	10 50	12 45
9 00	10 12	11 00	11 34	11 50	11 50	1 45

Connections at Lancaster for Columbia, Marietta, Wrightsville, Mt. Joy, Millersville, Manheim, Lititz, Quarryville, Strasburg, Ephrata, Terre Hill, Adamstown and intermediate Towns.

LANCASTER, Central Square, to COATESVILLE, DOWNINGTOWN, WEST CHESTER, PHILADELPHIA and intermediate Towns.

LAN-CASTER	COATESVILLE Arr.	COATESVILLE Lv.	DOWN-ING-TOWN	WEST CHESTER Arr.	WEST CHESTER Lv.	PHILA. 69th STREET
*3 45	**5 45	*5 45	*6 08	*6 48	7 15	8 24
*4 45	*6 45	7 00	7 30	8 07	8 15	9 24
5 45	7 45	8 00	8 30	9 07	9 15	10 24
6 45	8 45	9 00	9 30	10 07	10 15	11 24
7 45	9 45	10 00	10 30	11 07	11 15	12 24
8 45	10 45	11 00	11 30	12 07	12 15	1 24
9 45	11 45	12 00	12 30	1 07	1 15	2 24
10 45	12 45	1 00	1 30	2 07	2 15	3 24
11 45	1 45	2 00	2 30	3 07	3 15	4 24
12 45	2 45	3 00	3 30	4 07	4 15	5 24
1 45	3 45	4 00	4 30	5 07	5 15	6 24
2 45	4 45	5 00	5 30	6 07	6 15	7 24
3 45	5 45	6 00	6 30	7 07	7 15	8 24
4 45	6 45	7 00	7 30	8 07	8 15	9 24
5 45	7 45	7 50	8 13	8 48	9 15	10 24
6 45	8 45	8 50	9 13	9 48	10 15	11 24
7 45	9 45	9 50	10 13	10 48	11 15	12 24
8 45	10 45	11 00	11 23	11 58		

*Not run Sundays.

Connecting at 69th Street Terminal, Philadelphia, with the Market Street Elevated.

Time from 69th Street to Broad and Market Streets, 20 minutes.

to Chester County for use as a free public highway, for which the Lancaster turnpike company received $14,200.

Taylor immediately loaned $10,000 of this to the traction company for needed improvements to the trolley line. For nearly a year the Lancaster turnpike remained a paper company until it was dissolved on February 25, 1902.

There is no record of what Taylor had paid to get control of the turnpike company, but when its books were closed the traction company received $12,532 for its 1,034 shares of stock.

Taylor's next idea was an extension of the trolley line from a point a few miles east of West Chester to Westtown Boarding School, his alma mater. The school at the time was operating a stage coach to a nearby Pennsylvania Railroad station. Taylor wanted the school to put up most

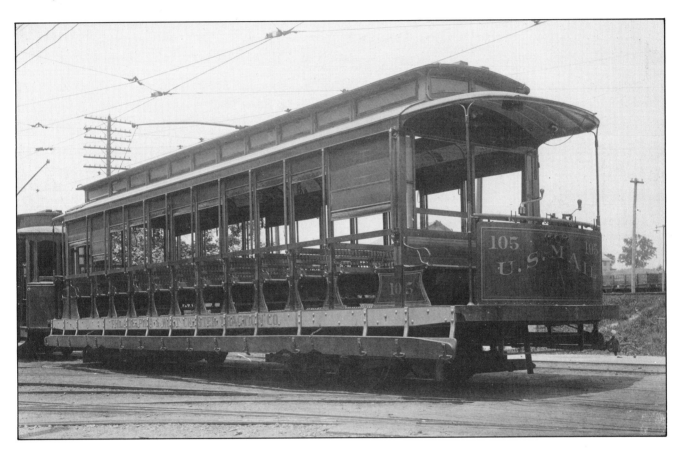

of the money for his extension, but the school vetoed that idea.

Thwarted again, Taylor next considered an extension from Newtown Square to Phoenixville via Malvern. Malvern is on the section of the Lancaster Pike which was still owned by the Philadelphia and Lancaster Turnpike Road Company, so this would have also provided an alternate route to reaching Coatesville.

With a population of 12,000, Phoenixville was slightly bigger than West Chester. Taylor estimated it would have taken two hours on the trolley between Center City Philadelphia and Phoenixville, however, twice the time required by the Pennsylvania or Reading Railroad trains.

Also, to get to Phoenixville would have meant crossing the Pennsy around Malvern, and the railroad would surely have fought this vigorously. Already the impudent little trolley cars were stealing business

Taylor purchased five large double-truck summer cars in 1900 which were an immediate hit with the passengers. Curtains could be pulled down to the floor if it rained. The motorman, however, had no protection. PST

away from the Pennsy because they charged only half as much for a ride
to West Chester and ran more often.

During 1901, the Philadelphia, Castle Rock and West Chester passed
resolutions to build 21 different branches and received official permission
from the commissioners of Haverford Township for several of them. The
extensions literally went all over the place, from Philadelphia to
Downington to Delaware. One would have even created a local loop line
within the Borough of West Chester.

Most of these extensions were never seriously contemplated, however.
They were filed chiefly so the traction company would have some legal
footing if other trolley companies tried to build anywhere around the
West Chester Pike area.

There was one group of promoters of paper traction companies in
particular that Taylor was interested in quashing. These men, all Phila-
delphians, had incorporated the Coatesville, Downingtown and West
Chester Street Railway Company; the Parkesburg and Coatesville; the
Coatesville and Western; the Coatesville and Downingtown; the Philadel-
phia, Wayne and West Chester; the Chester, Wayne and Norristown; the
Philadelphia, Media and Delaware, and the Philadelphia, Bridgeport and
Schuylkill, none of which ever got off paper.

The Coatesville and Downingtown Street Railway, however, filed suit
against Taylor's plan to build to Coatesville.

An Extension at Last

Determined to extend his West Chester line somewhere, Taylor finally
settled on Ardmore, a thriving town on the main line three miles from
Llanerch, and part of the area that the Pennsylvania Railroad considered
its own private fiefdom.

Since the Philadelphia and West Chester Traction Company could not
legally construct lines, a new corporation had to be formed.

If the new company were a regular electric railway company, it would
lack the right of eminent domain and might run into the same problem
that had killed the proposed Coatesville spur. If it were a company with a
steam railroad charter, however, it would build where it pleased and then
be leased to the traction company and electrified before it opened.

Uncertain of the legality of doing this, Taylor wrote to S. Davis Page, a
founding partner of Page, Allison and Penrose and the traction
company's attorneys for several years. Page replied that he saw "no difficulty in building under such general railroad law."

So on May 14, 1901, the Ardmore Railroad Company was chartered
with Taylor as president. Electricity for the line was to be purchased
from the traction company in return for all the profits of the Ardmore
Railroad. This would have given the traction company complete control,
just as it had over the Philadelphia, Castle Rock and West Chester.

The New York City engineering firm of Ford, Bacon and Davis was
hired to build the extension and provide the cars, and the connecting
switch at Llanerch was installed on June 5. Ford, Bacon and Davis would
get "five percent of the entire total cost of all materials and labor," plus
$250 a month for supervisory services.

The men behind all of the Coatesville area paper trolley companies
declared that they, too, wanted to build a line between Philadelphia and
Ardmore, and on June 10 they formed the Philadelphia, Devon and West
Chester Street Railway. It immediately filed suit against the Ardmore

Railroad Company, charging illegal construction of a trolley line under the guise of a steam railroad charter.

The case dragged throughout the summer, and the state attorney general's office finally declared the Ardmore Railroad Company's charter illegal and asked that it be revoked. But by that time the Ardmore Railroad was only a paper company. It was finally dissolved in 1904.

Wasting no time, Taylor incorporated the Ardmore and Llanerch Street Railway Company on June 18, 1901, as soon as he suspected trouble.

The new company was promptly leased to the traction company, and construction began in November. The first trolleys began running every 30 minutes on May 30, 1902.

The route was partly side-of-the-road running, partly private right-of-way and partly street running. It was originally single-track all the way to the end of the line at Sheldon Lane and Elm Avenue in Ardmore, where a small temporary station was built.

The contract with Ford, Bacon and Davis also called for three new passenger cars, which arrived in time to inaugurate the Ardmore service. Although they were ordered in the name of the Ardmore and Llanerch Street Railway, they were lettered for Philadelphia and West Chester Traction Company and were always operated in through service from Ardmore to 63rd Street. They were Nos. 14-16. They cost $12,300 each and seated 40 passengers.

The Ardmore and Llanerch company also ordered a snow sweeper and a work car in 1902, and another work car and two more big open cars—Nos. 106-107—the following year. The open cars cost $10,300 each.

When Taylor took over the traction company, its power generating plant at Llanerch was in poor condition and there was insufficient power on the western portion of the West Chester line. Taylor ordered new

Nos. 14-16 were obtained for the Ardmore line in 1902. The elegant little cars included smoking compartments. Historical Society of Pennsylvania

equipment for the powerhouse, which was installed in April 1900. But he underestimated the seriousness of the situation. During the summer of 1900 only half-hour service could be operated between Newtown Square and West Chester, and in September the new generator blew out under the strain. No cars ran west of Newtown Square for about a week until additional equipment could be secured.

Although the powerhouse was only 500 feet from the Newtown Square branch of the Pennsy, no siding had been installed and the traction company had been using wagons to haul coal from the railroad to the powerhouse.

Taylor had a short elevated railroad siding constructed so coal could be unloaded into little hand-pushed, narrow-gauge coal cars, then wheeled

Opening day on the Ardmore line was a gala occasion. Scarcely another passenger could have crowded aboard No. 14 at Llanerch Junction on May 29, 1902. Wilbur P. Hall

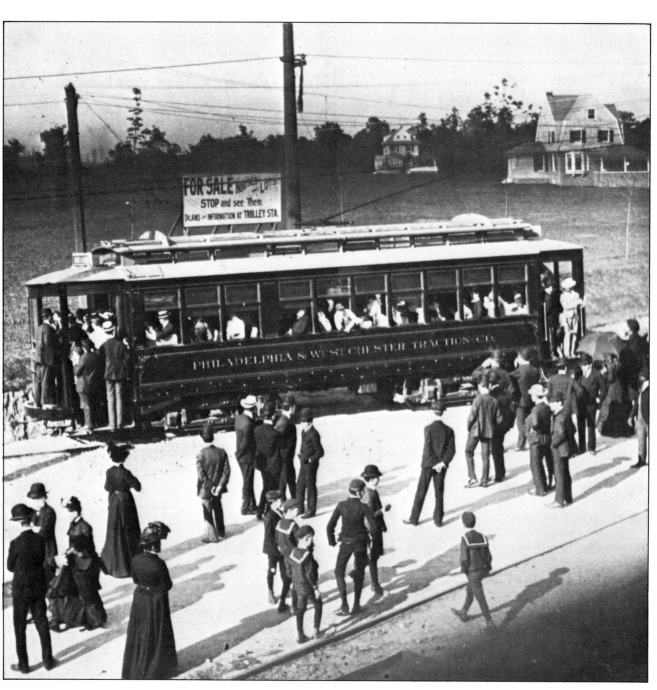

View along the new Ardmore line west from Llanerch. The dirt trail parallel-ing the tracks on the left is Darby Road. Cattle guards were common along the route. Wilbur P. Hall

The exact same location five years later. The trolley line has been double-tracked and Darby Road substantially improved. The cattle guards are still in use. PST

directly into the adjacent boiler room. This saved much time and manpower.

By 1901 Taylor's father, Charles S. Taylor, had bought 70 acres of land in Llanerch at the junction of the Ardmore and West Chester lines and was preparing to build houses.

Taylor saw this as another way of making more money, by selling electricity to homeowners. He incorporated the Eureka Light, Heat and Power Company on September 9, 1901, bought some land across West Chester Pike from the carbarn and constructed a large stone building in which to generate the electricity.

Eureka was authorized to "supply light, heat and power by electricity to the public in the Township of Haverford." As a sideline Eureka ran a small stable and a grass-cutting business.

In 1906 Taylor incorporated three more electric companies, called Marple Light, Heat and Power Company; Upper Darby Light, Heat and Power Company; and Square Light, Heat and Power Company. On December 5 they were all merged into the new Eureka Electric Light, Heat and Power Company. President of these companies and of the merged company was H. Hayes Aikens, a close friend of Taylor and vice president of the traction company.

Eureka was soon serving thousands of customers all the way from 63rd Street to Newtown Square and from Ardmore to Garrettford. Eureka produced excellent profits which sometimes amounted to as much as 80 percent of its gross earnings. The company was sold in 1912 to United Gas Improvement Company.

The trolleys originally required an hour and 25 minutes to run to West Chester, but Taylor chopped that down to an hour and 12 minutes beginning October 7, 1903, by relocating some sidings and improving the condition of the track.

No. 15 posed with its crew at the original Ardmore Terminal at Sheldon Lane and Elm Avenue, about one-third of a mile short of Lancaster Pike.
Wilbur P. Hall

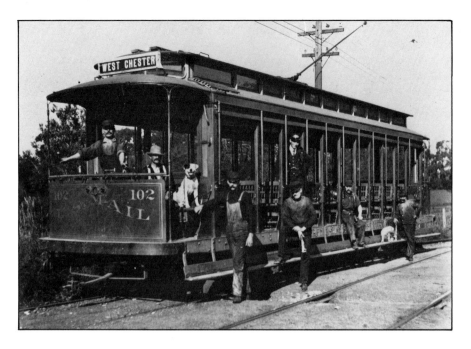

Maintenance men posed at the Llanerch carbarn with No. 102 in 1903. The dog on the front seat was the Llanerch mascot. When he died, he was stuffed and mounted in a glass case in the dispatcher's office. He remains in existence more than 80 years later. Collection of Hilda Shadel Lucas

There were many accidents on the West Chester line in the early years, some amusing and some serious.

On November 7, 1900, a motorman lost control of car No. 11 and it ran 50 feet off the end of the rails at 63rd Street. It had to be towed back onto the track.

Beware of Bulls and Cows

Car No. 8 was charged by a bull near Newtown Square on September 15, 1900. There is no record of what happened to the animal, but No. 8 had two holes in its dash where the horns struck. The same car hit a cow near Milltown 11 days later.

Single-truck car No. 100 killed a bull in West Chester on October 4 of the same year, and on January 25 of the next year No. 8 collided with a horse and wagon at Manoa Road crossing, killing the horse and smashing the wagon to bits.

Quite a few animals were killed or injured when they challenged the trolleys.

One day a bull disputed the right-of-way with a trolley near Llanerch. The bull took a firm stand on the tracks and the trolley slowed, stopped, then crept forward a few feet. The bull charged, and the small car rocked when the animal slammed into it. The bull repeatedly butted the front end of the trolley, then finally gave up and wandered off, leaving the battered car and shaken passengers to continue their journey to West Chester.

Two cars running in opposite directions on single-track crashed into each other at Castle Rock on October 4, 1900, injuring 11 passengers.

Car No. 13 seemed particularly prone to bad luck. On its way out to West Chester on July 13, 1902, a drunken man who had been arrested by a local constable was put on board so he could be taken to the West Chester jail. He became rowdy, and several male passengers sat on him until the car reached the jail. On its return trip out of West Chester, No. 13's motorman applied the brakes suddenly in an attempt to avoid hitting a dog. The heavy application of brakes caused a fire to flare up, igniting the floor of the car. It was put out by the crew and passengers, but a few minutes later it broke out again, this time burning out the controller and igniting the motorman's coat.

Drunks seemed to find the roadbed a particularly comfortable or handy place to take a nap, and in 1899 three of them were run over by trolleys and killed.

Motormen at the time were working 12 hours daily, seven days a week. They received 17 cents an hour, out of which they had to purchase their own $15 uniforms.

Revenue increased from $86,000 in 1899 to $147,000 by 1903, resulting in very small profits in 1901—for the first time—and 1903. There was a $4,200 deficit in 1902.

Taylor had not been devoting his time solely to the traction company during the early years. In 1902 he and some friends incorporated the New Jersey and Hudson River Railway and Ferry Company. He served as president of that company for a decade, building up a system which included a ferry line from 130th Street in New York City to Edgewater, New Jersey, and an electric railway from Edgewater to Englewood, Paterson, Hackensack, Passaic and Newark. The company was finally purchased by the giant Public Service Corporation, which ran trolleys in cities all over New Jersey.

Taylor also helped to reorganize several other trolley companies during his early years in the business, including the Trenton and New Brunswick Railroad Company, the New Jersey Short Line Railroad Company, the

The Ardmore line was extended to the downtown business district of Ardmore in 1905, and a large terminal was constructed on Lancaster Pike across the street from the Pennsylvania Railroad station. The Ardmore Terminal building included a separate waiting room for women. The trainshed contained two tracks and gates to control the crowds. PST

Meadville (Pa.) Railway, the Montgomery (Ala.) Traction Company and the Riverside (N.J.) Traction Company. He also served as president of the Riverside company for a while.

Things still weren't going nearly as well financially for the Philadelphia and West Chester as Taylor had expected. It was going to take a long time, he could now see, before the traction company was safely out of the red and producing good dividends. And he was determined to be around when this finally happened.

So on February 11, 1903, Eastern Securities Company was created, further complicating the traction company's already intricate corporate setup.

Eastern Securities was formed by Taylor and his closest friends, including Hayes Aikens. The purpose of the new company was to gain control of the traction company so that nobody could vote Taylor out of office, and it was a very clever move. It also eventually provided much larger profits for Taylor and the other owners of Eastern Securities than they would have gotten through normal dividends.

Taylor offered a stock trust certificate bearing five percent annual interest in return for each share of traction company stock turned in to Eastern Securities. The guarantee was that if Eastern Securities should ever fail to meet its interest payments, the traction company stock would be returned to its original owners. So the stockholders really had nothing to lose, but a nice guaranteed annual dividend to gain.

View of the trainshed from the rear. Each platform was long enough for two cars, but there was seldom more than one car at a time at Ardmore. PST

Most of them jumped at this opportunity because their traction company stock had been paying no dividends. Much of the stock was exchanged immediately, and within three years all of it was held by Eastern Securities.

This meant Eastern Securities now controlled the entire railway and turnpike operation. The scheme would initially cost Taylor and his friends a great deal of money because Eastern Securities was obligated to pay the five percent annual interest on the trust certificates whether or not it received any dividends from the traction company.

The dividends in those early years never nearly amounted to the interest payments, so Taylor and his associates had to dig into their own pockets for quite a bit of money.

If the traction company should not eventually prove to be profitable, the men behind Eastern Securities would not only lose the money they had put up but they would also have to return the stock to its original owners. It was a tremendous risk, but it was to pay off handsomely because in the later prosperous years it meant that any profits over five percent were divided only among the few men who controlled Eastern Securities.

The Reason for the Risk

Taylor apparently was willing to take such a big risk because always in the back of his mind was that elevated railway to Center City Philadelphia. In fact, the Market Street Elevated Passenger Railway Company had been incorporated in 1901 and acquired by the Philadelphia Rapid Transit Company in 1902. By mid-1903 construction was underway.

To be ready for the elevated, the traction company engaged in a grandiose rebuilding and expansion program.

The West Chester line was double-tracked between 63rd Street and Manoa in 1905 and the substation at Ridley Creek seven miles east of West Chester was converted into a second powerhouse which opened on

Form No. 7-a.   5 M.   12-28-05

Philadelphia & West Chester Traction Co.
SCHEDULE IN EFFECT JANUARY 1, 1906
Between Ardmore and 63d and Market Streets

Leave 63d and Market Sts.	Arrive Ardmore
8 minutes after each hour	28 minutes after each hour
23 minutes after each hour	43 minutes after each hour
38 minutes after each hour	58 minutes after each hour
53 minutes after each hour	13 minutes after each hour

Leave Ardmore	Arrive 63d and Market Sts.
31 minutes after each hour	50 minutes after each hour
46 minutes after each hour	5 minutes after each hour
1 minute after each hour	20 minutes after each hour
16 minutes after each hour	35 minutes after each hour

Small cards were issued in 1906 showing 15-minute service to Ardmore. PST

Opposite:
Looking toward 63rd Street from the top of Naylor's Run Bridge in Beverly Hills on the Collingdale line in 1906. The entire line was originally built as single-track, but was graded for double-track. PST

One of the original West Chester line cars crosses Naylor's Run Bridge on the Collingdale line in 1906. The bridge carries the trolleys over the Pennsylvania Railroad's Newtown Square branch. PST

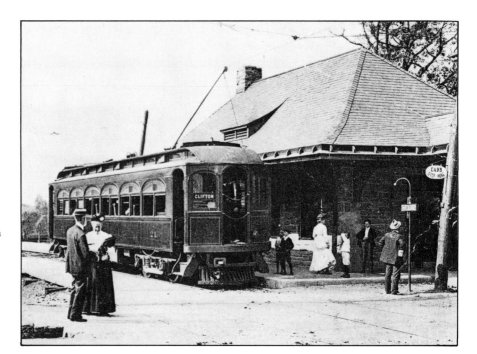

The original end of the line at Clifton in 1906, with one of the new interurban cars. Collection of Thomas Smith

The big stone station at Clifton included rest rooms and a newsstand. The outbound platform was made of wood because the traction company expected to remove it soon when the line was double-tracked. PST

The first of the large stone stations was built in 1906 at Lansdowne Avenue on the Collingdale line. An interurban car is approaching the station, heading for 63rd Street. PST

Trolleys reached the end of the line in Collingdale on July 15, 1907. Passengers could transfer there to cars of the Philadelphia Rapid Transit Company to reach Darby, Chester and Media. PST

June 1, 1905. A dangerous curve on a steep hill in front of the new power-house was eliminated by a bridge, and a siding was built so that freight cars hauled from Llanerch to Ridley Creek could dump their coal directly into the boiler room.

Two hundred workmen were hired to put the track between Manoa and West Chester into first-class shape, including some minor track realignments. These improvements cost $215,000, raised through the sale of Philadelphia and West Chester Traction Company four percent bonds. One of the curves realigned was at Castle Rock and required the purchase of a small piece of land. Shimer owned the land, and sold it only after the traction company granted him and his wife, Elizabeth, lifetime trolley passes.

The Ardmore line was double-tracked from Llanerch to Manoa Road, and the route was extended slightly more than a quarter of a mile further to Lancaster Pike in Ardmore's business district, just across the street from the Pennsylvania Railroad station.

Originally the trolleys followed Darby Road all the way to Eagle Road in Oakmont, then cut cross-country on a series of sharp curves to Merwood station. This trackage was eliminated in 1905 in favor of a more direct route between South Ardmore and Merwood.

The new two-track Ardmore terminal, described as "one of the handsomest electric railway stations in the country," was opened September

The first of the big interurban cars arrived in 1906, and were easily the most impressive trolley or interurban cars operating in the Philadelphia area. Nos. 17-23 were built by Brill.
Haverford Township Historical Society

1, 1905, and trolleys began running to Ardmore every 15 minutes on December 15 instead of every half hour.

The terminal building was made of "Pompeiian brick, with Indiana limestone trimmings" and a roof of Spanish tile. The interior included an ornate fireplace, rest rooms, a separate waiting room for women, a newsstand and a ticket office.

The trainshed could hold four cars, and iron gates were installed so that the stationmaster could keep those leaving the trolleys separate from those waiting to board.

The running time from Ardmore to 63rd Street was cut from 24 to 20 minutes.

The *Street Railway Journal* at the time called the improvement project "a noteworthy example of what can be done in making over a dilapidated, nonpaying country trolley road into a successful, modern interurban property."

Impressed with what they saw, 95 residents of Gladwyne, a few miles east of Ardmore, petitioned Taylor to extend the trolley line. But Taylor had his sights on much bigger things.

By mid-1903, with construction finally underway on the elevated railway that Taylor had been counting on, the traction company took a step toward the most important project it would ever conceive: 69th Street Terminal.

The interiors featured high-backed leather seats and empire-style ceilings with inlaid woods. Haverford Township Historical Society

The interurbans included train doors between cars so they could eventually be operated over the Market Street Elevated to Center City. Collection of John Gibb Smith, Jr.

The first section of the elevated which was being constructed by PRT was to run from 15th Street west to 23rd Street in a subway; then it would surface and go over the Schuylkill River on its own bridge, becoming an elevated structure over Market Street at 30th Street. From there it would continue out to 63rd and Market Streets, where a huge terminal was to be constructed. West Philadelphia was still devoted largely to farmland, and the elevated was a bold step toward developing the entire area.

Stage two of the plan called for an extension eastward from 15th Street to the Delaware River, where ferry boats carried vacationers to Pennsy and Reading trains in Camden for a journey to seashore resorts on the Atlantic coast.

Taylor planned to build a new high-speed trolley line in an entirely different direction from the existing West Chester and Ardmore routes, and he wanted to terminate all three lines in a spacious new building that would be shared by the elevated trains and the high-speed electric trains of the Philadelphia and Western Railroad, which was then under construction. He expected to also enter into a trackage rights agreement with PRT so he could run his trolleys over the elevated directly into Center City.

The first of these projects to be completed was the high-speed trolley to Collingdale. Taylor first considered a route along Marshall Road, but ultimately chose to follow Garrett Road.

Again it was necessary to incorporate a separate company to construct the line, so on May 10, 1904, the Philadelphia and Garrettford Street Railway Company was created. Its original charter called for only a one-mile route from West Chester Pike and Garrett Road to the point where the Pennsy's Newtown Square branch crosses Garrett Road. Extensions were filed soon afterward giving the company the right to build nearly four miles further to Collingdale.

It took a year to secure the permission of all the landowners over whose property the trolley would run, and construction finally began in August 1905. The Philadelphia and Garrettford was leased to the Philadelphia and West Chester Traction Company on October 23, 1905, just as the Ardmore and Llanerch had been.

The Collingdale Division was not going to be like the two previous lines. It would be like nothing, in fact, in all of southeastern Pennsylvania. It would be a fast, interurban-type line and it would have the best equipment that could be purchased.

Construction progressed rapidly, and on March 15, 1906, the line began operating from 63rd Street to Baltimore Pike in Clifton, a distance of 3.3 miles. A single car provided service every 30 minutes.

By June the big, elegant interurban cars—Nos. 17-23—that Taylor ordered from the J.G. Brill Company had arrived, and they started running to Clifton on June 15. Four of them were purchased in the name of the Ardmore and Llanerch Street Railway and three in the name of the Philadelphia and Garrettford. They were 45-foot wooden cars sheathed with steel below the windows, and they were fast.

The outside was a "rich maroon" with gold striping, according to a contemporary account.

"It is hard to conceive a more graceful arch than is embodied in the upper part of the twin windows and the ventilator sashes," said a trade journal of the era. "The effect is heightened by the arched row of green art glass of the window heads.

"In the interiors a light-green tinted dome of empire style, decorated

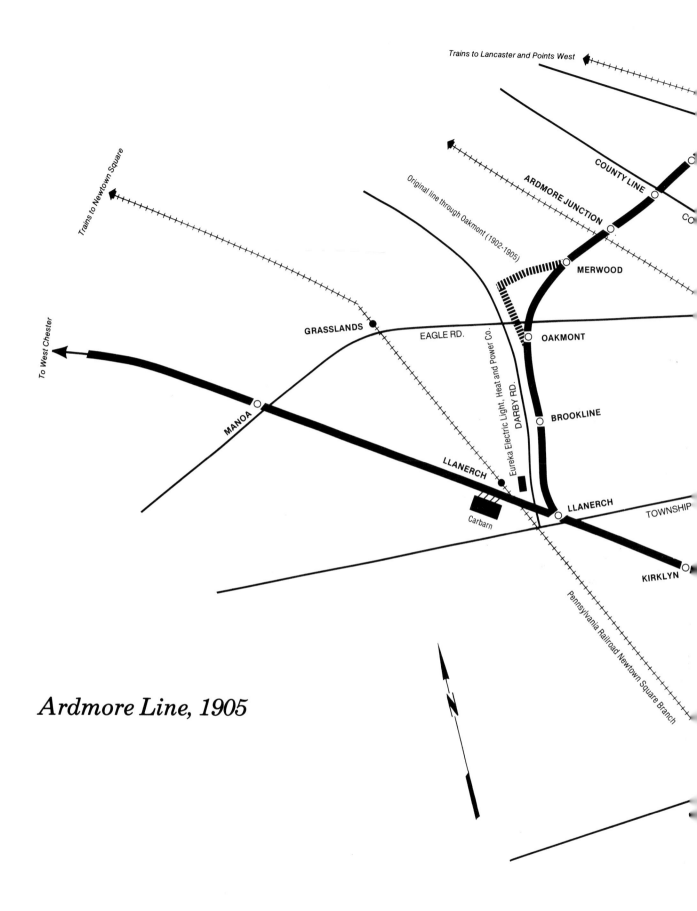

Ardmore Line, 1905

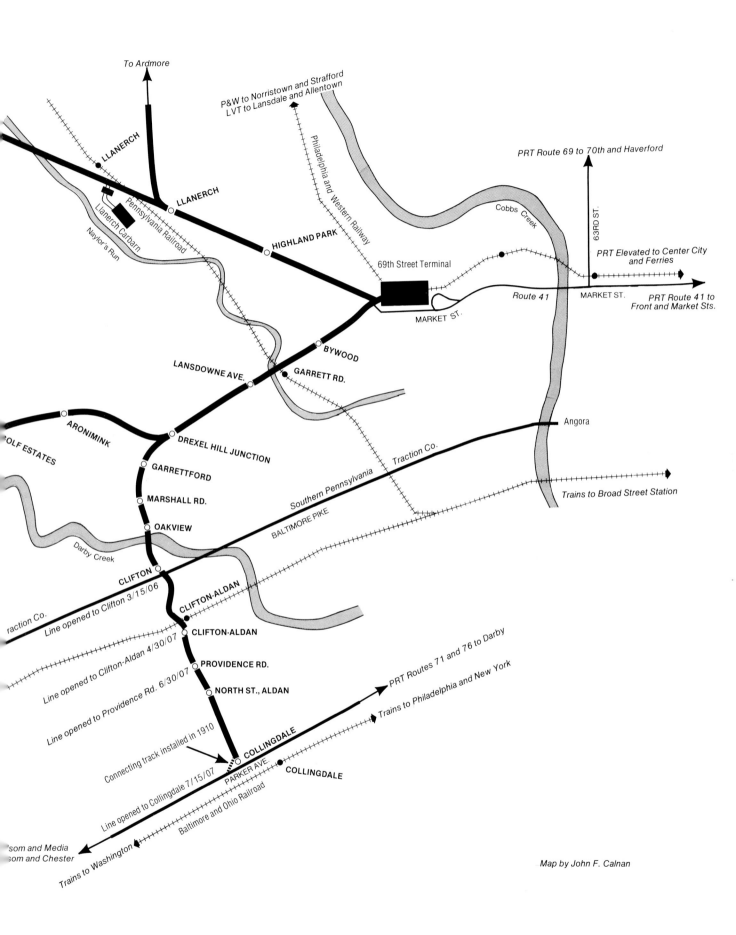

To Ardmore

P&W to Norristown and Strafford
LVT to Lansdale and Allentown

PRT Route 69 to 70th and Haverford

LLANERCH

LLANERCH

Philadelphia and Western Railway

Cobbs Creek

Llanerch Carbarn

63RD ST.

Pennsylvania Railroad

LLANERCH

PRT Elevated to Center City
and Ferries

Naylor's Run

HIGHLAND PARK

69th Street Terminal

Route 41

MARKET ST.

PRT Route 41 to
Front and Market Sts.

MARKET ST.

BYWOOD

LANSDOWNE AVE.

GARRETT RD.

Angora

ARONIMINK

GOLF ESTATES

DREXEL HILL JUNCTION

GARRETTFORD

Southern Pennsylvania

Traction Co.

Trains to Broad Street Station

MARSHALL RD.

OAKVIEW

BALTIMORE PIKE

Darby Creek

CLIFTON

raction Co.

Line opened to Clifton 3/15/06

CLIFTON-ALDAN

CLIFTON-ALDAN

Line opened to Clifton-Aldan 4/30/07

PROVIDENCE RD.

PRT Routes 71 and 76 to Darby

Line opened to Providence Rd. 6/30/07

NORTH ST., ALDAN

Trains to Philadelphia and New York

Connecting track installed in 1910

COLLINGDALE

Line opened to Collingdale 7/15/07

PARKER AVE.

COLLINGDALE

som and Media
som and Chester

Baltimore and Ohio Railroad

Trains to Washington

Map by John F. Calnan

This view at Highland Park about 1905
shows how well maintained both the
trolley line and the turnpike were. PST

To West Chester

Collingdale and Media Lines, 1913

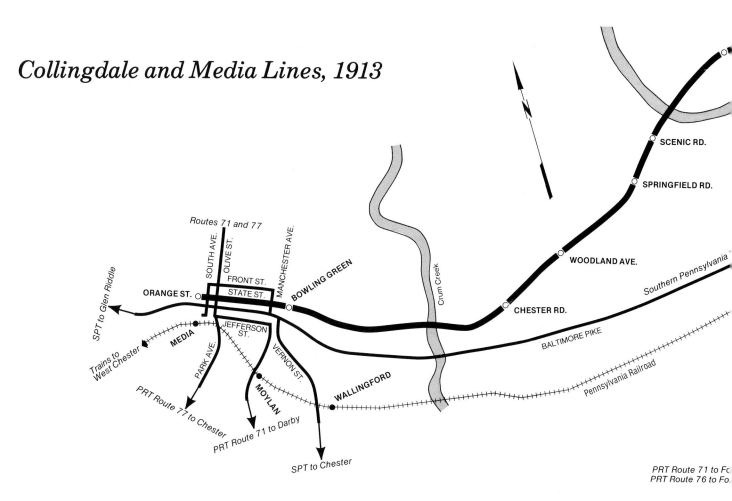

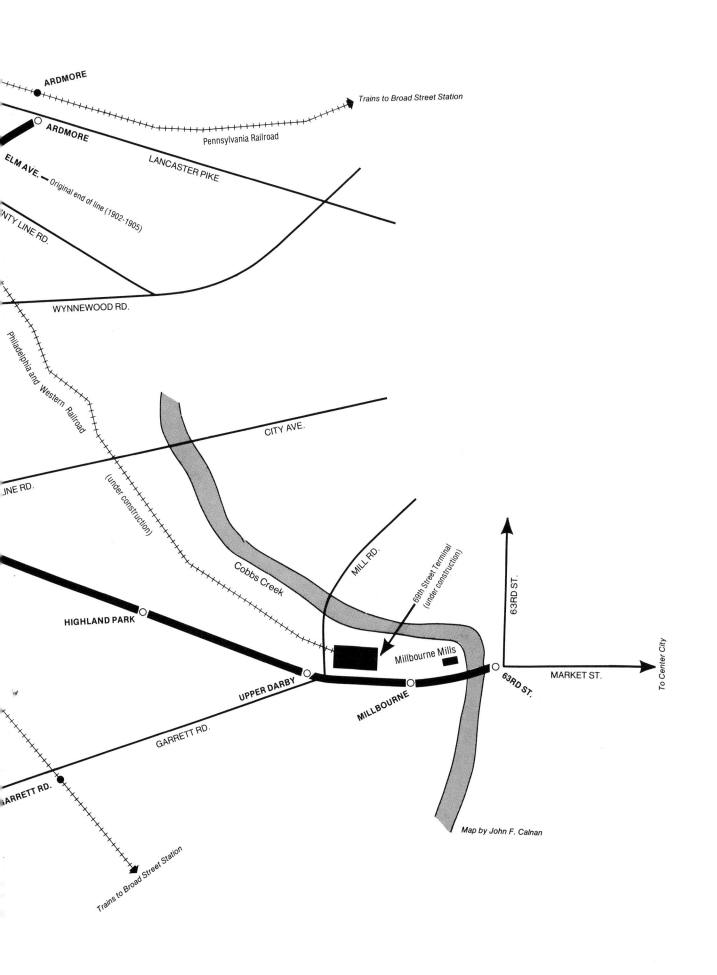

ARDMORE

ARDMORE

Trains to Broad Street Station

Pennsylvania Railroad

ELM AVE. — *Original end of line (1902-1905)*

LANCASTER PIKE

...NTY LINE RD.

WYNNEWOOD RD.

Philadelphia and Western Railroad

CITY AVE.

...INE RD.

(under construction)

Cobbs Creek

MILL RD.

69th Street Terminal
(under construction)

63RD ST.

HIGHLAND PARK

Millbourne Mills

MARKET ST.

To Center City

UPPER DARBY

63RD ST.

MILLBOURNE

GARRETT RD.

...ARRETT RD.

Trains to Broad Street Station

Map by John F. Calnan

with gold festoons of ribbon, contrasts pleasantly with the rich dark red of vermilion woods, which constitute the interior finish.''

The interiors included high-backed seats finished in dark-brown leather and separate smoking compartments. Actually, the cars were slightly smaller versions of traditional steam railroad coaches. The cars were truly the best that money could buy, and they made PRT's streetcars look shabby by comparison.

Taylor and the passengers were highly pleased with the posh new cars. They increased ridership and brought prestige to the traction company. The next year nine more of them—Nos. 24-32—arrived. These were built by Jewett and were longer than the Brill models. These big new interurban cars now covered most trips on all three rail lines. They helped to completely change the image of a trolley company which only a few years earlier had been running slow, uncomfortable little four-wheel cars, and they were remarkably successful in attracting passengers.

All of these cars had high platforms with traps that had to be lifted to permit passengers to climb up the steps, much like steam railroad cars. And all the cars had doors in the ends of them so passengers could walk from one car to another. The width of the cars and the floor height were the same as the elevated cars PRT had ordered so that the traction company would be ready whenever an agreement was reached permitting its cars to run over the elevated.

On August 6, 1906, a large stone station was opened at Lansdowne Avenue on the Collingdale line, and on October 7 an even bigger station

Seven more of the interurbans—Nos. 24-30—arrived in 1907, three feet longer and with four more seats than the 1906 cars. Originally, the Brill and Jewett interurbans were not lettered with the company's name, but had gold striping. The small windows in the clerestory opened for ventilation. PST

Two more cars arrived later in 1907, Nos. 31-32. They were again three feet longer, seating 56 passengers and making them the longest cars the traction company ever operated. Collection of Harry P. Albrecht

was opened at Clifton. A similar stone station was completed at Oakmont on the Ardmore Division on August 18. Many more of these attractive, substantial stations were built at additional locations over the following 20 years, and most were still in use in the 1980s.

The Clifton line was entirely on private right-of-way. It paralleled Garrett Road to Drexel Hill, then struck south cross-country to Clifton. It included two spectacular bridges, one over the Pennsy at Naylor's Run and one over Darby Creek in Oakview. Although the line was initially single-track, it was built with the expectation of soon double-tracking it the whole way. The double-track was added in stages over the years.

The arrival of the interurban cars permitted the immediate scrapping of all the single-truck cars. No. 6 remained on the roster until about 1930 because it had been turned into an emergency car. PST

Empty Seats Pay Off

Taylor made it a policy to run many more cars than he needed to on all three divisions. His policy was summed up by a 1906 magazine article: "The receipts per mile of track are high, but the receipts per car-mile and per car-hour are low because of the liberal service given. Cars are operated at certain times of the day with many empty seats, and a better showing could be made by curtailment in the present schedules.

"But the management adheres to the present frequent and fast service, confident in the belief that the 'empty seat' question will work out its own solution and the proportion of unoccupied seats to total carrying capacity, which may now seem extravagant, will gradually be reduced by the very fact that the public is rapidly realizing that comfortable empty seats are available."

This remained the basic policy of the traction company for several decades, and it paid off.

A half-mile extension from Clifton to the Clifton-Aldan station of the Pennsy was opened April 30, 1907, and trolleys began running every 20 minutes.

PRT was originally planning to end the elevated on property belonging to the Burd Orphan Asylum on the south side of West Chester Pike just west of Cobbs Creek. That meant the traction company's cars would have had to continue running along the side of West Chester Pike between Garrett Road and the elevated terminal near 63rd Street. Taylor preferred to have the terminal built at the intersection of West Chester Pike and Garrett Road because he felt it would enable a bigger and better joint facility to be built that would include plenty of space for the traction company's cars and for future growth.

PRT agreed to extend its line if Taylor would secure the necessary right-of-way for the elevated west of 63rd Street. A further stipulation

The interurbans operated in two-car trains when traffic was heavy. A train inbound from Ardmore approaches Brookline station. Collection of Andrew W. Maginnis

was that the Collingdale line must be at least partially operating by the time the elevated was ready to begin service.

Taylor had trouble obtaining the consent of some property owners, and in early 1905 he received a letter from PRT's president threatening to end the elevated at 63rd Street unless Taylor hurried up and got the land. Taylor hurried.

Part of the elevated ran across land belonging to Millbourne Mills, and John Sellers, Jr., and his brother William, who owned the mill, each received lifetime passes on the elevated in return for their cooperation. John Sellers, however, died in 1905.

In early 1905, Taylor drew up an agreement that would have enabled his cars to run over the elevated to Front and Market Streets. The traction company would have purchased three-quarters of all the cars needed to maintain through service to Ardmore and West Chester, and PRT would have bought the rest. PRT employees would have operated the trolleys on the elevated, but the traction company would set the schedules. The trolleys would have run express from Center City to 69th Street.

PRT rejected the agreement.

Taylor kept trying, however, and as late as 1914 he was still buying new cars that would have been compatible with the elevated.

Taylor Builds a Terminal

The big 69th Street Terminal was actually three separate stations, all of them built in the middle of farmland. Cows had grazed there until construction began.

Construction of 69th Street Terminal in early 1907. The traction company's five-track, stub-end station is nearing completion. Under construction in the foreground are the loop tracks for the elevated trains. Collection of Ronald DeGraw

PRT built the main structure with a high-ceilinged waiting room and offices on a mezzanine level. Passengers went down steps to reach the two loading tracks. The elevated trains began running between 69th Street and 15th Street on March 5, 1907, and were extended to the Delaware River ferries in September.

On the north side of the terminal was the end of the line for Philadelphia and Western trains to Strafford, which began running on May 22, 1907.

Tacked onto the western side of the PRT building was the ornate five-track trainshed of the traction company, each track long enough for three cars. At the end of the tracks was a big lobby which connected with PRT's main waiting room. Over top of the lobby were the new offices of the traction company. When the traction company opened its part of 69th Street Terminal on April 30, 1907, all trolleys except those in the early hours of the morning began and ended their runs there. A shuttle car continued to operate along West Chester Pike from 63rd Street to Garrett Road and free transfers were issued for it.

The terminal and the Collingdale line were financed through the sale of $800,000 in Philadelphia and Garrettford bonds. Hayes Aikens was technically president of the Philadelphia and Garrettford, although all of its business was conducted by the traction company and Eastern Securities owned all 160 shares of its stock.

A new schedule went into effect with the opening of the terminal, and the following June 30 the Collingdale line was extended another quarter mile from Clifton-Aldan station to Providence Road in Aldan. The final extension to MacDade Boulevard (then Parker Avenue) in Collingdale opened July 15, 1907, making the line a total of five miles long.

Cars then ran every 15 minutes to Collingdale and the trip took 16 minutes. The running time was increased to 18 minutes a year later. There was three-quarters of a mile of street running through Aldan, but the rest of the line was on private right-of-way. The street running occurred because of still another encounter with the Pennsylvania Railroad. The trolley had to cross the railroad's West Chester branch at

The front of the terminal a month after it opened. Collection of Harry P. Albrecht

All three of these photographs were
taken from exactly the same location,
in 1900, 1908 and 1984. PST

Clifton-Aldan, and Taylor took the easy way out. He ran the trolley line underneath the railroad in the middle of Springfield Road, which was already grade separated from the railroad. There was nothing the Pennsy could do to block the trolleys.

To provide sufficient power for the expanding system, a cable from a PRT substation at 56th and Market Streets was connected to the Collingdale line on July 12, 1907, with the traction company paying PRT for whatever power it consumed.

A large fireproof brick carbarn was built in Llanerch behind the old barns, opening December 1, 1907. With six storage tracks, two repair tracks and two paint tracks, the barn could hold more than two dozen cars. Entry from West Chester Pike to the new carbarn was through one of the old barns, which were retained for storing supplies. The new barn and shops cost $50,000, and another $100,000 was spent at the same time to increase the powerhouse capacity.

The Market Street Elevated lived up to all of Taylor's expectations in creating additional traffic for the traction company's line. Business boomed, and two-car trains frequently had to be run to handle the crowds. On the West Chester division, extra cars were sometimes attached to regular trains as far as Larchmont. There they would be cut off and coupled onto the next eastbound train. To handle the increased traffic, five more Jewett cars—Nos. 33-37—arrived in 1912.

Taylor still wasn't finished expanding his system. Additional double-track was installed on the Ardmore and Collingdale lines, and on May 20, 1912, a local car began running between the terminal and Drexel Hill on weekdays during the evenings to relieve the traffic on the Collingdale cars. On Sunday afternoons business was particularly heavy, and often a regular Collingdale train would carry an extra car as far as Clifton.

View of the traction company's train-shed two months before it was completed. The Philadelphia and Western Railroad terminal is under construction on the right. Collection of Harold E. Cox

The timetable that became effective
when 69th Street Terminal opened
showed service to West Chester every
30 minutes, to Clifton every 20 minutes
and to Ardmore and 63rd Street every
15 minutes. Ronald DeGraw

View of the junction outside 69th
Street Terminal in 1907. West Chester
Pike is in the foreground. The tracks
going out of the photo at the right are
to West Chester and Ardmore. The
tracks switching off and running
behind the building in the center of the
photograph go to Collingdale. Notice
the semaphore signals. On the left, the
tracks slanting toward the bottom of
the photo lead into the five-track
trainshed. The other tracks are the
original main line to 63rd Street. The
building on the left is the Bond Feed
Store, which served as the Upper
Darby freight station. PST

ARDMORE DIVISION

Running time, Westbound, 20 minutes, Running time, Eastbound, 19 minutes

DAILY

Leave 63d Street ....5.40 A. M.	Leave Ardmore...........5.48 A. M. Runs to 63d St.
Leave 63d Street .... 5.55 A. M.	Leave Ardmore..........6.03 A. M. Runs to 63d St.
Leave 63d Street ....6.10 A. M.	
Leave 63d Street..........6.25 A. M.	Leave Ardmore ....6.18 A. M. Runs to 69th St. Cars run to 69th Street every fifteen minutes there-after until 11.18 P. M.
Leave 69th Street ....6.40 A. M.	
Cars run from 69th Street every fifteen minutes there-after until 11.40 P. M.	Leave Ardmore ....11.18 P. M. Runs to 69th St.
Leave 69th Street ....11.40 P. M.	Leave Ardmore .... 11.33 P. M. Runs to 63d St.
	Leave Ardmore .... 11.48 P. M. Runs to 63d St.
Leave 63d Street .... 11.55 P. M.	Leave Ardmore .... 12.03 A. M. Runs to 63d St.
Leave 63d Street .... 12.10 A. M.	Leave Ardmore .... 12.18 A. M. Runs to 63d St.
Leave 63d Street .... 12.25 A. M.	Leave Ardmore .... 12 33 A. M. Runs to 63d St.
Leave 63d Street .... 12.40 A. M.	Leave Ardmore .... 12.48 A. M. Runs to 63d St.
Leave 63d Street .... 12.55 A. M.	
Leave 63d Street .... 1.10 A. M. Runs to Llan-erch only	Leave Ardmore .... 1.03 A. M. Runs to Llan-erch only
	Leave Ardmore .... 1.18 A. M. Runs to Llan-erch only

NOTE:—Additional trips will be added as traffic requires.

First car leaves Llanerch for West Chester at 4.40 A. M.   First car leaves Llanerch for Ardmore at 5.34 A. M.
First car leaves Llanerch for 63d Street at 5.09 A. M.   Last car leaves 63d St. for Llanerch at 1 10 A. M.

All West Chester and Ardmore cars run via Llanerch.

Running time between Llanerch and 63d St., Eastbound, 10 minutes, Westbound, 9 minutes.

First car leaves Newtown Square for 63d St. 5.54 A. M.   Before 6.35 A. M. and after 11.43 P. M. all regular cars run to 63d St.

There were almost twice as many passengers riding during the summer months, and frequently three times as many people rode on Sundays as on weekdays. In those days before automobiles and television, pleasure travel was an important source of income for trolley companies.

The regular schedules called for 15-minute service on the Collingdale and Ardmore divisions and 30-minute service to West Chester. There were no additional trips scheduled for peak periods, but two-car trains were run as needed during rush hours and on weekends. On busy summer weekends, cars ran to West Chester every 15 minutes as needed.

With the 69th Street Terminal and the Collingdale line completed, Taylor decided to next expand to Media. He had selected a route that would branch off from the Collingdale line at Drexel Hill and run completely cross-country to the little town of Media, the county seat of Delaware County.

A contractor was hired in May 1912 and construction began that summer. By January the track was finished and two months later the electrical system had been installed.

The Media line was built to even higher standards than the Collingdale division. It required heavy cuts and fills and was the most expensive of the four lines to construct. No hills on the line exceeded three percent, and there was a maximum curvature of five degrees. A new substation was built at Aronimink.

The line was completely graded for double-track, and bridge abutments were all made wide enough to accommodate a future second track, although in the 1980s some of the line remains single-track.

When it opened on April 1, 1913, there were only two small villages—Aronimink and Springfield—between Drexel Hill and Media. The route was 8.5 miles long from the 69th Street Terminal to the end of the line at State and Orange Streets in Media. There was three-quarters of a mile of

69th Street Terminal a few months after it opened in 1907. The entrance to the waiting room of the Market Street Elevated was through the three arches on the right. The entrance to the traction company's waiting room was through the single door in the section of the building adjacent to the five-track trainshed. Both companies had their offices overhead. In the foreground is West Chester Pike and the double-track line to 63rd Street. PST

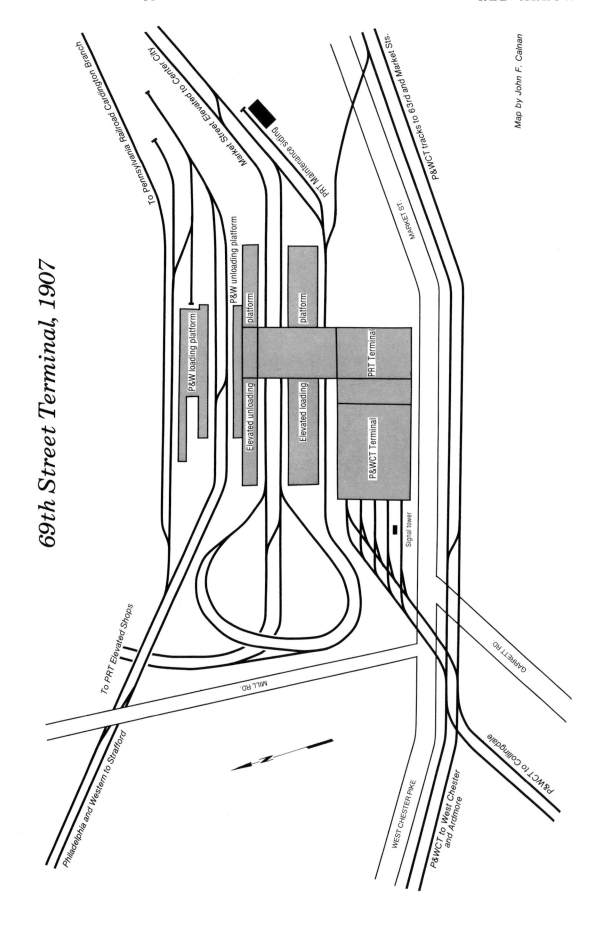

69th Street Terminal, 1907

Map by John F. Calnan

Ornate train gates kept passengers off the platforms until trolleys were ready to load, similar to steam railroad practice. Collection of Harold E. Cox

The waiting room of the Market Street Elevated included a lunch counter, a newsstand and a ticket office in 1908. PRT offices were on the second floor, and a skylight brightened the waiting room. The entrance to the traction company's waiting room was through the doors on the right. Collection of Harold E. Cox

THE PHILADELPHIA and West Chester Traction Company issued a "Code of Rules for Government of Trainmen and Operation of Trains." The first edition appeared in 1907, and employees were expected to commit to memory all of the regulations it contained and to carry the book with them while on duty.

A few of the more interesting rules follow:

—SPECIAL: Should any trainman who has been in the employ of the Company more than six months, suffer from want of money by reason of prolonged sickness or death in his immediate family, or for any other reason beyond his control, he should make his necessities known to the superintendent or the president of the Company, who will treat any such information as strictly confidential and give the matter proper consideration.

—STEAM RAILROAD CROSSINGS: Train must be brought to a stop at a safe distance, approaching steam railroad crossings at grade, and motorman must not proceed until conductor has gone ahead to the center of crossing, looked both ways, and given the "Come Ahead" signal. Before starting, the motorman will look back to see that no passengers are getting on or off; and in no case proceed even after conductor's signal has been given, until he has also examined the crossing and satisfied himself that steam cars are not approaching.

—FATAL ACCIDENTS: In the event of a fatal accident, it will not be necessary to blockade the line awaiting the arrival of the coroner or any other official. If an accident occurs where it is impossible to carry the body to a place of shelter and security where it will be properly cared for, motorman and conductor will put the body on the train and convey it to some suitable place.

—WIRE THIEVES: Trainmen will keep a sharp lookout along the road for any suspicious wagons at night. Wire thieves frequently stand their wagon on a cross road a short distance from the main road. Trainmen will immediately notify the dispatcher on duty in case any strange and suspicious wagons are seen.

—COLLECTION OF FARES: Conductors must not give over five pennies to any one person in change. Should passenger object to pennies conductor must take them back and give other change.

—U.S. MAIL: Mail trains will not wait over 30 seconds for mail at 63rd and Market Streets or West Chester. Under no condition will mail train wait for mail which is not ready on schedule time at the various post offices along the line. If P.R.T. mail car does not arrive in time for regular mail train, the next westbound West Chester train leaving will carry the mail.

—POLICEMEN AND MAIL CARRIERS while in uniform will be carried free of charge within the borough limits of West Chester.

—VENTILATION: Special care must be taken to regulate ventilators according to number of passengers and condition of weather; always keep train so ventilated that the air will be cool and pure. Endeavor to comply with all reasonable demands from passengers regarding doors, windows and ventilators. Raise and lower windows and curtains on request of passengers. Curtains on open trains must be kept rolled up when not in use.

Revised editions of the rulebooks were issued about every ten years, and the first rulebook for bus operators appeared in 1929.

street running at the end of the line, but for the rest of the distance the trolleys sped through scenic, wooded countryside. Because of its speed, the line was referred to as the "Media Short Line."

A combination trolley-elevated ride from Center City to Media was a few minutes quicker than the Pennsy's Media trains and less than half the price. For the first few years, cars ran to Media only every half hour because of light traffic. Two more large interurban cars built by Jewett— Nos. 38-39—were obtained for use on the Media line, costing $12,000 each.

Except for a short extension to be built four years later, the traction company's rail network was now complete.

The Media Division featured a high bridge in Smedley Park that was built for double-track. This portion of the line was still single-track in the mid-1980s. PST

An interurban sporting white flags
arrived at Drexel Hill Junction on a
test run in early 1913, shortly before
the Media line was completed. PST

A 1921 aerial view of Llanerch shows
the entire carbarn area. The large barn
at the right was built in 1907 and
served as the traction company's only
maintenance and indoor storage facility
for railcars until 1971. Five snow
sweepers and plows are lined up on the
track adjacent to the barn. The two
older carbarns appear at the bottom of
the photo. These were later converted
for use as bus maintenance facilities.
The large smokestack is connected to
the powerhouse. The Pennsylvania
Railroad's Llanerch passenger station
is at the bottom left, and West Chester
Pike is the principal road running
diagonally through the picture. PST

Chapter 4

Castle Rock Park

MANY TROLLEY AND INTERURBAN LINES at the turn of the century built amusement parks as a means of attracting more passengers and making extra money. The parks were often built in a remote location that was difficult to reach without taking the trolley.

The Philadelphia and West Chester Traction Company's park was a notable failure, lasting only seven seasons. The traction company built its park in the rocky terrain of Castle Rock, 10.5 miles west of 63rd Street. John Shimer, while he was in control of the company, liked the idea of having an amusement park located in the area where he had grown up.

He was so excited about it, in fact, that he had the traction company buy 38 acres in April 1895, nearly four years before the trolley line was actually extended as far as Castle Rock.

In the meantime, Shimer opened a temporary park along the line at Broomall, six miles west of 69th Street. Broomall Grove had a dancing pavilion, refreshment stands and picnic grounds. The traction company hired an orchestra to play each day except Sundays during the summer months, and the park was a moderate success. Receipts sometimes went as high as $300 for a busy summer weekend and, of course, most passengers reached the park by riding the trolleys.

The traction company named its new glorified picnic grove Castle Rock Park. It was officially opened on Memorial Day, May 30, 1899, shortly after the trolleys began running through to West Chester. Broomall Grove had been closed the previous fall and most of its attractions moved to Castle Rock.

The new park featured a shooting gallery, a small restaurant, a dance pavilion, weekend cornet concerts, a dairy that served "dainty luxuries," picnic grounds along Crum Creek, fishing in the well-stocked stream, hammocks and swings, and fireworks and balloon ascensions on the Fourth of July.

A few cottages were even built for persons who wanted to get away from the bustle and heat of the city and spend a quiet week or two in the country.

"Several amusements have been engaged for the summer, but the merry-go-round is lacking," A. Merritt Taylor, the traction company's new president, told his board of directors on May 10, 1899. "Every effort has been made to secure one for the park without avail and, as no park on a trolley line has ever been successful without a merry-go-round, I believe it is necessary to have it. I request the board to authorize the purchase of a merry-go-round upon the most favorable price to be obtained."

The board readily gave its permission, and a steam-powered merry-go-round was installed before the summer was over.

Round-trip excursion tickets to Castle Rock were sold at 63rd Street and at West Chester for 20 cents, and hundreds of people flocked to the park. The park was open only from Memorial Day through Labor Day each year.

An orchestra was hired for $180 a month to play on Saturday afternoons and every night except Sundays. A "noted cornetist," William

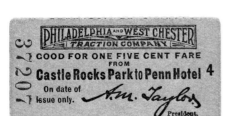

Organized picnics were popular summer events at Castle Rock Park. The traction company probably used its influence with suburban milk shippers to arrange this picnic. PST

Second Annual Picnic

of the

Philadelphia Milk Shippers' Union

will be held at

Castle Rock Park

Delaware County, Pa., on

THURSDAY, AUGUST 21, 1902

You and your friends are cordially invited to be present. The public will be welcome. Take Market St. car to Sixty-third and Market Sts.; there change to the car of the PHILADELPHIA & WEST CHESTER TRACTION COMPANY, which runs direct to **Castle Rock Park.**

An exceptional opportunity is offered of hearing matters of vital interest to farmers discussed by able men who will speak on this occasion; also attractive music, which will be rendered by a Regimental Band.

❧ ❧ SPEAKERS ❧ ❧

Hon. Leonard Rhone   *Hon. Thos. S. Butler*
on "The Unjust Taxation of Farms"   has promised to make an address

Hon. Thos. J. Phillips   *Hon. Wayne McVeagh*
on "Needed Legislation and How to   has promised to be present, if at all
Secure It"   possible, and make an address

Rev. J. D. Detrich
on "The Farmer of the 20th Century, or How to Keep
20 or More Animals on 15 Acres"

Participants may either provide their own lunch or secure it at the restaurant on the grounds

Lower Merion News, Ardmore, Pa.

Northcott, was engaged at $25 a week. He perched on a high rock and played on weekends.

Castle Rock was a picturesque, wooded hillside area studded with rock masses and honeycombed with caverns, the ideal setting for children's games. It had a legendary history as the hideout for highwayman Sandy Flash, a local Robin Hood who terrorized the sparsely populated area around Newtown Square during Revolutionary War days.

His real name was James Fitzpatrick, and he deserted George Washington's forces after he was flogged as punishment for an offense. He deserted to the British, and took particular delight in robbing Whig tax collectors and local taverns. He reportedly gave some of his loot to

The seven double-truck open summer cars were popular with passengers traveling to Castle Rock Park. PST

Nos. 106-107 remained in excursion service until the early 1920s, used principally on the West Chester Division. PST

poor families in the area, and lavished expensive presents on his female acquaintances. He was finally caught while dallying with a farmer's daughter during the robbery of a local farmhouse, and he was hanged in 1778 in Chester.

For years afterward people searched through his rock-infested hideout looking for the gold he had allegedly hidden away.

Shimer as a boy must have played among these rocks. His family's house was just across West Chester Pike on what is now Shimer Lane.

The traction company tried valiantly to promote its scenic little park, and dozens of Sunday School and company picnics were arranged, with

A Geographic Society picnic at Castle Rock Park in 1901 poses in front of some of the spectacular rock formations. PST

A covered bridge on West Chester Pike and a water tower to replenish the traction company's sprinkler car stood at the entrance to Castle Rock Park in 1901. PST

special open trolley cars assigned to carry the crowds.

The park was described by a local newspaper as "even more beautiful than Willow Grove Park," the big amusement facility operated by the Philadelphia Rapid Transit Company, although this was wild exaggeration.

"The beautiful and romantic grounds may eventually possess a fine hotel built on a high point," mused one writer.

In glowing rhetoric, a "Summer Programme" which was distributed all along the trolley line and throughout Philadelphia just prior to the park's opening told readers that a visit to Castle Rock would "fill a long-felt want on your part."

"The people of Philadelphia have heretofore been at a great disadvantage owing to the fact that in taking a ride on the trolley cars they have been unable to get fairly out into the country without going many miles through city streets and the built-up sections of the suburbs," explained the brochure. "Now they can board one of the palatial cars of the Philadelphia and West Chester Traction Company, and from the time they get on until the time they get off they are rushing up over hills, through the woods, down through valleys, and along beautiful shaded streams enjoying the most beautiful scenery to be found within a radius of 30 miles. There is always a breeze on the cars and the company's sprinkler will prevent the usual dust nuisance.

"Castle Rock Park is located just halfway between Philadelphia and West Chester and will be the most popular resort of all the people living

This view just east of Castle Rock Park shows the primitive state of West Chester Pike. The covered bridge over Crum Creek is at the bottom of the hill. The slightest rain turned the highway into a muddy morass, but the trolleys sped on. PST

in the cities at each end of the road. Nature has endowed this wonderful park with attractions which could not be produced by artificial means. The rocks tower above the treetops and inspire every visitor with wonder.

"Pleasures heretofore only enjoyed by the more fortunate are now within the reach of all. Send your family out on a picnic someday during the week and try a ride over the entire line, and take dinner or supper at the Green Tree Hotel, which is immediately opposite the end of the tracks in West Chester. The meals are exquisite and the hotel is highly recommended to the most particular."

The biggest event of the season for several years was the "Grand Harvest Home and Tri-County Reunion," a gala day crammed full of speeches, contests, dancing, eating and a minstrel show. Games for children and adults included the traditional greased pig race, a wheelbarrow race and a sack race.

Castle Rock was a long distance from downtown Philadelphia, however, and in those days before the Market Street Elevated was operating it required an hour and a half or more for many city dwellers to reach the amusement park. The PRT's huge Willow Grove Park and the Fairmount Park Transportation Company's Woodside Amusement Park were much closer and much bigger, so Castle Rock Park suffered from a chronic lack of patronage. West Chester area residents could easily and more quickly travel to Lenape Park, which was a more substantial amusement park than Castle Rock.

Castle Rock Park closed in 1905, and two stone crushers were erected to break up the big rocks to provide ballast for the expanding trolley system.

Sunday Schools continued to hold picnics in the area. Finally in 1926 the traction company sold most of the park area to William Bricker, a real estate developer who planned to build a "model community." Nothing much came of Bricker's dream, and even today there are only a few homes in the area.

Chapter 5

Buses Supplement the Rail Cars, 1914–1929

CONTINUING INCREASES IN RIDERSHIP required the purchase of five more Jewett cars in 1914, Nos. 40-44. Now there were 28 of the big interurban cars, and they handled all of the service on the four lines. Open car Nos. 106-107 were still used during the summer months for special events such as picnics.

All of the earlier cars had been removed from passenger service.

To accommodate its expanding car fleet, the traction company in 1915 purchased three acres of land in back of the Llanerch carbarn across Township Line Road and extended its storage tracks across the highway.

With the beginning of World War I in 1914 and the great expansion of the shipbuilding companies located in Chester, Pennsylvania, Taylor laid plans the following year to extend his Collingdale line a third of a mile further south to Chester Pike in Sharon Hill. There passengers could transfer to the Southern Pennsylvania Traction Company's double-track line running from Darby to Chester.

Taylor had some difficulty constructing an underpass where the trolleys would cross the Baltimore and Ohio Railroad between Collingdale and Sharon Hill, delaying the opening of the extension until August 1, 1917. Taylor and Southern Pennsylvania set up a joint fare of 13 cents from Chester to 69th Street Terminal.

Taylor had not been able to build his Collingdale trolley line without fighting off other trolley companies in the area, and some of them threatened to compete with the traction company's cars.

Interstate Railways Company, a syndicate that operated systems in Chester and Wilmington and controlled Southern Pennsylvania Traction, attempted several times to extend its lines to a connection with the Market Street Elevated. Interstate formed the Sharon Hill and Upper Darby Street Railway in 1906 to build from Chester Pike to 69th Street via Clifton Avenue, Baltimore Pike, Wycombe Avenue, Union Avenue, Marshall Road, Long Lane and Garrett Road, but the proposed line had trouble getting a franchise from the Borough of Lansdowne.

Interstate was persistent, however, and by January 1909 Lansdowne's borough council seemed ready to grant the franchise. This line would have served some of the same territory as Taylor's traction company, and would have been a menace to any future extensions of the Collingdale line. The Interstate line would also have provided a direct route from 69th Street Terminal to Chester. So Taylor also asked for permission to run a line between the Terminal and Lansdowne, chiefly in an effort to block the proposed Sharon Hill and Upper Darby company.

Taylor's line would have branched off from the Collingdale division at Lansdowne Avenue, then gone straight south for about two miles on

FRIENDS' EXCURSION
West Chester--Chesapeake City
Sixth-day, Sixth Month 18, 1915
Leave Gay & High Sts., West Chester, at
6.15 A. M.
Tickets, $1.35
Not Including Car-fares across Philadelphia
69th St. Terminal to West Chester
Good on Special Cars Only

- -

FRIENDS' EXCURSION
6th Mo. 18, 1915
Ericcson Line Steamer
Chesapeake City to Philadelphia

- -

FRIENDS' EXCURSION
6th Mo. 18, 1915
Ericcson Line Steamer
Philadelphia to Chesapeake City
Leave Pier 3, foot of Chestnut Street,
Philadelphia, 8 A. M.

- -

FRIENDS' EXCURSION
6th Mo. 18, 1915
Phila. & W. C. Traction Company's Line
West Chester to 69th St. Terminal
Good on Special Cars Only

The traction company offered excursion trips from West Chester to Chesapeake City, Maryland. The four-part ticket was good for fares on charter trolleys and on the Ericcson Line steamboats. Passengers had to pay the five-cent Market Street Elevated fare in cash. The date on the tickets has been written in an unusual manner in deference to the Quakers who sponsored this trip. Chester County Historical Society

Lansdowne Avenue to the Pennsy's Lansdowne station. This would have been a slow, streetcar-type operation.

Borough council appeared to be leaning more toward granting a franchise to Interstate, so Taylor obtained an injunction forbidding the borough from giving anybody the franchise. And he went to court in an effort to have the charter of the Sharon Hill and Upper Darby revoked on the grounds that it hadn't started construction within the time limit specified by law.

Interstate abandoned the Sharon Hill and Upper Darby proposal and came up with another scheme. The Terminal Railway Company was organized, and instead of building on Lansdowne streets this company would construct a line through East Lansdowne to 69th Street.

Interstate's Baltimore Pike line from Media to Philadelphia crossed the Collingdale division at Clifton, and Southern Pennsylvania had tried unsuccessfully to block the traction company from crossing its tracks there during construction in 1906.

It appeared as if Taylor had finally been beaten, but he came up with another idea that completely defeated Interstate.

Running along MacDade Boulevard at the end of the Collingdale line was PRT's Darby to Chester single-track trolley line. Taylor and PRT put in a connecting switch between the two lines in 1910 and signed an agreement that through service between 69th Street Terminal and Chester would begin whenever either company requested it. Such a route would have been much faster than the one proposed by Interstate via East Lansdowne. The through service never started, but just the threat of it was sufficient to discourage Interstate, which withdrew from the battle.

The traction company's proposed extension into Lansdowne took a few years to die, and was still being considered by Taylor as late as 1914. In 1918, Taylor briefly considered the possibility of a spur from Aldan to Morton.

A High Point Is Reached

But the era of electric railway construction had reached an end. The short extension to Sharon Hill in 1917 was to be the traction company's last track expansion. It is interesting to note that 1917 was also the year that electric railway mileage throughout the United States reached its peak of 44,000 miles. Many trolley lines should not have been built, and they were abandoned as soon as the automobile started competing during the 1920s, with electric railway mileage dropping to below 35,000 by 1930.

When the trolley was in its heyday, however, hundreds of miles of suburban routes existed throughout the Philadelphia area, providing numerous connections for the traction company's cars.

At West Chester, the West Chester Street Railway Company operated three lines. One was a local line in West Chester, and another ran to Lenape Park and Kennett Square, where connections could be made to Wilmington or West Grove. The third route ran to Downingtown and Coatesville on essentially the same routing that the traction company had attempted to build in 1900. This line was opened in 1902. Connections could be made at Downingtown for trolleys to Lancaster, operated by Conestoga Traction Company. Joint timetables were issued in 1910 showing service from 69th Street to Lancaster, for the use of those inter-

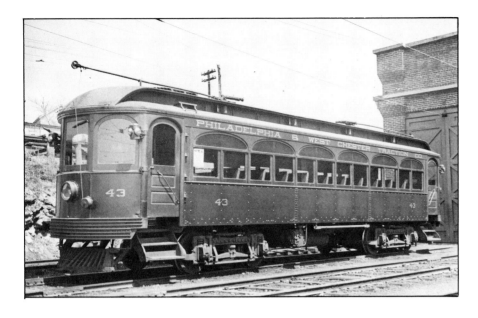

Five of these handsome cars were acquired from Jewett in 1914. No. 43 posed in front of the Llanerch carbarn. Collection of Fred W. Schneider, III

ested in spending four hours and 15 minutes on a trolley journey.

A connecting switch between the traction company and the West Chester Street Railway was installed at Gay and High Streets in West Chester, but was seldom used. The traction company's open cars reportedly operated through to Lenape Park on occasion, and West Chester Street Railway's cars sometimes ran to the race track just east of West Chester on the traction company's line.

The Ardmore division crossed underneath the Philadelphia and Western's trains at Ardmore Junction. The P&W ran a branch to Strafford and another to Norristown. The Lehigh Valley Transit Company's high-speed interurban trains operated over the P&W to Norristown, then continued on to Lansdale, Quakertown and Allentown. At Ardmore, the Pennsylvania Railroad offered important connections to the western part of the Main Line, Harrisburg, Pittsburgh, Chicago and other points.

The extension to Sharon Hill opened on August 1, 1917. The crew and some well-attired passengers posed at the station shortly after it opened. PST

The Sharon Hill division also connected with the Pennsy at the Clifton-Aldan station of its West Chester line. Sharon Hill trolleys connected with Southern Pennsylvania at Baltimore Pike for Angora and Media and at Chester Pike for Darby and Chester. The PRT trolleys at MacDade Boulevard ran to Darby, Chester and Media. The Baltimore and Ohio's Collingdale Station was not far from the traction company's line; trains ran to New York and Washington.

The traction company's route to Media became the sixth trolley line to serve the little town. PRT operated a route between Media and Chester and another from Media to Darby. Southern Pennsylvania ran between Media and Angora and between Media and Chester, and had another line from Media west to Glen Riddle.

The connections for the traction company's lines were extensive, and were well patronized in the early years. None of these other trolley lines except the P&W had been built to the high standards of the traction company's line, however, and all of them fell easy prey to the rapidly encroaching automobile during the 1920s. Some of these connecting lines had been abandoned by the late 1920s, and every one of them except the P&W and Lehigh Valley Transit was gone by the end of the Depression.

The traction company's lines, however, continued to prosper, largely because they were well built and well operated.

Through all of this growth and prosperity, Taylor still found time to continue engaging in outside activities. He served as Philadelphia's transit commissioner from July 1912 through July 1913, during which time he turned out a massive report recommending a long-range plan for

Steam shovels and tiny horse-drawn wagons aided in the construction of the Sharon Hill extension in 1917. PST

transportation construction in Philadelphia. Included were a subway under Broad Street, a Center City loop subway that would have run under Arch, 16th, Locust and 8th Streets, and elevated lines to Darby and Frankford. The 25-mile rapid transit system would have cost an estimated $57 million. Taylor was named as the first director of the new Department of City Transit in 1913, serving until January 1915. He refused to accept any salary for his work with the city.

Taylor was appointed as director of passenger transportation and housing for the United States Shipping Board's Emergency Fleet Corporation on April 3, 1918. He was in charge of securing adequate passenger transportation to 180 shipyards on the Atlantic and Pacific coasts, the Gulf of Mexico and the Great Lakes. He resigned January 31, 1919.

"Taylor was possessed of great determination and tenacity, but was nevertheless a man of very conservative temperament, modest by nature, and unassuming, yet with a keen sense of humor," according to the Encyclopedia of American Biography.

He was also a demanding but humane employer. On scores of occasions, the traction company paid the medical bills of employees, loaned them money for good causes and performed other charitable gestures in the days before unionization.

The traction company issued this map in 1917, showing the extensive network of connecting trolley lines that existed. Within 15 years, most of these lines had been abandoned. PST

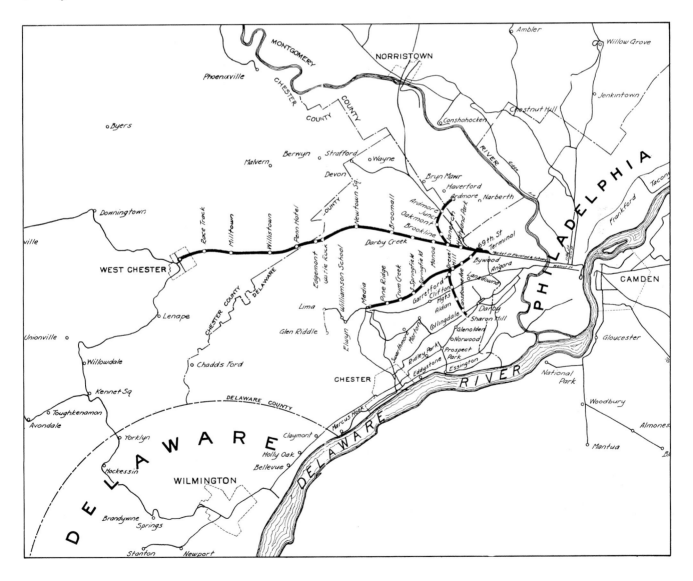

The minutes of a board of directors' meeting in 1914 read: "It was reported to the Board that Motorman Harry Knott was in a critical physical condition, which made it necessary for him to be operated on at the American Stomach Hospital, that his finances were in no shape to stand this extra expense," and that the company would "render such financial aid deemed necessary." There are dozens of similar entries.

Money was loaned to many employees at low interest rates. Grants were made to the widows of faithful employees. A cryptic notation in the corporate minute books for 1917 stated: "A contribution of $50 to William Welsford, Day Maintainer at 69th Street Terminal, on account of domestic troubles, was confirmed."

Turkeys were given to all employees at Thanksgiving, and the employees knew that they could count on the traction company to help them in time of financial need.

One of the few people who didn't like Taylor was Thomas E. Mitten, president of PRT. Mitten took control of PRT in 1911, and he deeply resented the appointment of Taylor as the city's transit commissioner and director of city transit. Mitten considered Taylor a suburban upstart encroaching on PRT territory. Mitten also didn't like subway and elevated lines, at least not when they were built by the city and PRT was charged high rentals. Taylor's reports, of course, recommended the construction of new subway and elevated lines.

In November 1919, Mitten decided to play a little game with the traction company, much to Taylor's extreme displeasure. Mitten began turning back many Market Street Elevated trains at 63rd Street, instead of running them through to 69th Street. This proved of considerable inconvenience to the traction company's passengers, and both the traction company and the Philadelphia and Western complained to the

For some long-forgotten reason, employees staged a fake holdup aboard No. 20 in front of the Llanerch carbarn about 1920. PST

Pennsylvania Public Service Commission. Mitten claimed he did it because it saved three percent of the elevated's operating costs.

The 63rd Street turnbacks continued until the Market Street line was extended to Frankford in 1922.

During the period of expansion for the traction company, the turnpike was not being neglected. In 1909 a section of the road was rebuilt and paved with a hard surface for the first time. The portion through Millbourne was rebuilt in 1914 as well as part of the road just east of Newtown Square.

The center-door cars which arrived in 1919 originally sported gold striping and used simple red marker lights. Later paint schemes eliminated the striping. The original marker lamps were replaced by new ones that included red, green and white colors. PST

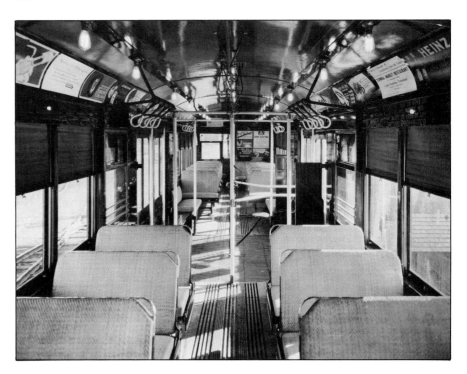

The interiors of the center-door cars were very plain compared to what the company's passengers had become accustomed to, featuring wood slat floors, bare light bulbs and rattan seats. PST

By 1918 the turnpike between 63rd Street and Llanerch was a hard-paved, two-lane highway. The toll was two cents per horse per mile. Autos were charged the same if they had only two seats, but the toll was doubled if they were four-seaters. Bicycles were charged one cent per mile.

The construction of 69th Street Terminal made it necessary to move Toll Gate No. 1 from the intersection of West Chester Pike and Garrett Road; it was relocated about two blocks west of 63rd Street in Millbourne. Gate No. 2 remained at State Road and Gate No. 3 was at Llanerch. No. 4 was still just east of Darby Creek and No. 5 remained just east of Larchmont.

Receipts from the turnpike under Taylor's management increased from $7,675 in 1900 to $10,441 in 1910. The turnpike company again began declaring dividends in 1904, after not paying them for more than 20 years. After 1910 dividends usually amounted to about six percent a year. Nearly all of this money, of course, went to the traction company, since it held all but 41 shares of the turnpike company's stock.

The Toll Road Bows Out

The profitability of the turnpike was to be short-lived, because on April 5, 1918, it was sold for $75,000 to Delaware County and the Pennsylvania State Highway Department. The legislature had passed a law in 1911 setting up a system of state highways, which included West Chester Pike. Under the law, any toll roads were to be condemned by the state.

The highway department dragged its feet, so a group of Delaware County residents formed the West Chester Pike Committee in November 1915 to urge the county to take over the turnpike. Eventually the purchase price was shared by the county and the highway department, and all the toll gates were closed. Repaving of the entire road began in 1919.

The sale of the turnpike created a strange situation since the turnpike company technically owned the trolley line from 63rd Street to Newtown Square. And the law under which the Philadelphia and West Chester Traction Company had been formed did not give it the right to purchase any of the lines it operated. The legislature therefore passed a special act in 1919 permitting the traction company to acquire the railway and franchises from the turnpike company. This was done on January 5, 1920, and at the same time the traction company agreed to purchase at $28.43 per share any turnpike stock still outstanding.

Another special act of the legislature allowed the traction company to acquire ownership of the trolley line between Newtown Square and West Chester from the Philadelphia, Castle Rock and West Chester Railway, which had long been only a paper company. This transfer also took place on January 5.

During 1917, its last full year of operation, the turnpike had receipts of $19,400. Its income had increased rapidly as more and more autos used the road. The turnpike company was formally dissolved on March 24, 1920.

More and more passengers were using the trolleys, also, and the 28 Brill and Jewett interurban cars were no longer adequate to handle the traffic. Taylor liked the Jewett Car Company's products, but Jewett was out of business by this time so the order automatically went to the J.G. Brill Company. Brill continued to build all of the traction company's cars until eventually it, too, went out of business.

The new cars—Nos. 45–54—were vastly different from the ornate old wooden cars that passengers had become used to. These cars were all steel and had center doors. The old interurbans had been very slow in loading and unloading because passengers could use only the single rear door except at terminal points. All departing passengers had to be off the car before new passengers could board, and the doors had to be hand operated by the conductors. They were designed for limited stop interurban service, but by this time the traction company's lines had become suburban trolley routes with frequent stops.

The new center-door cars had big wide sliding doors in the center of each side of the car that permitted two people to leave and two people to enter at the same time. The conductor sat on a collapsible stool near the

The traction company's original five tracks at 69th Street Terminal are visible in this 1921 photograph. Houses have been built all around the terminal, but no stores have as yet been constructed on 69th Street Boulevard. West Chester Pike, in front of the terminal, is in the process of being moved to the right by about 50 feet so that the terminal can be increased from five to eight stub-end tracks. At left are the maintenance shops for the elevated trains. PST

The expanded terminal opened in 1923 to accommodate the increased business on the traction company's rail lines. The first floor of the signal tower at the left was still standing in 1984. PST

doors and controlled them automatically. The new cars were much more efficient in handling crowds. Like the old cars, they had couplers so they could be operated in two-car trains as traffic required.

The center-door cars weren't nearly as fancy as the older cars. Their interiors were downright spartan, in fact, compared to the luxurious interurbans. They even had rattan instead of leather seats. The motorman sat tucked away in an enclosed cab at the front end of the car. The cars cost $17,500 each and arrived in 1919.

There were now many more trolleys operating in and out of 69th Street Terminal than when it had been built in 1907, and the traffic had simply outgrown the five-track facility. The terminal was at times impossibly congested, and it became apparent that ridership would continue to grow.

There was really no place the terminal could be expanded to, however. On the north side was the loop for elevated trains, on the east side was the PRT part of the terminal, on the south side was West Chester Pike

The front of the 69th Street Terminal looked like this after the 1923 expansion of the trolley area. The vehicles parked in front of the main steps are taxicabs. The double-track in the foreground leads to the 63rd and Market Streets freight terminal. PST

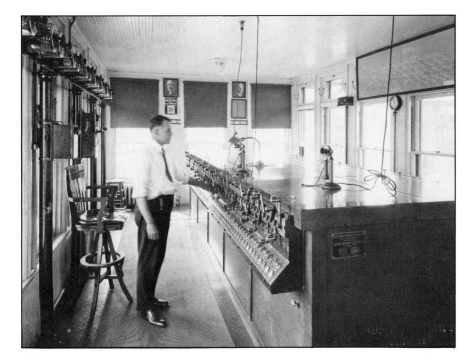

The complicated arrangement of switches at the expanded terminal was controlled from the second floor of the signal tower. A track plan appears in the upper right. PST

Horse-drawn wagons were still prevalent when this photo of the junction just outside the terminal was taken in 1925. The terminal is at the right and the freight tracks are in the foreground. Collection of Harry P. Albrecht

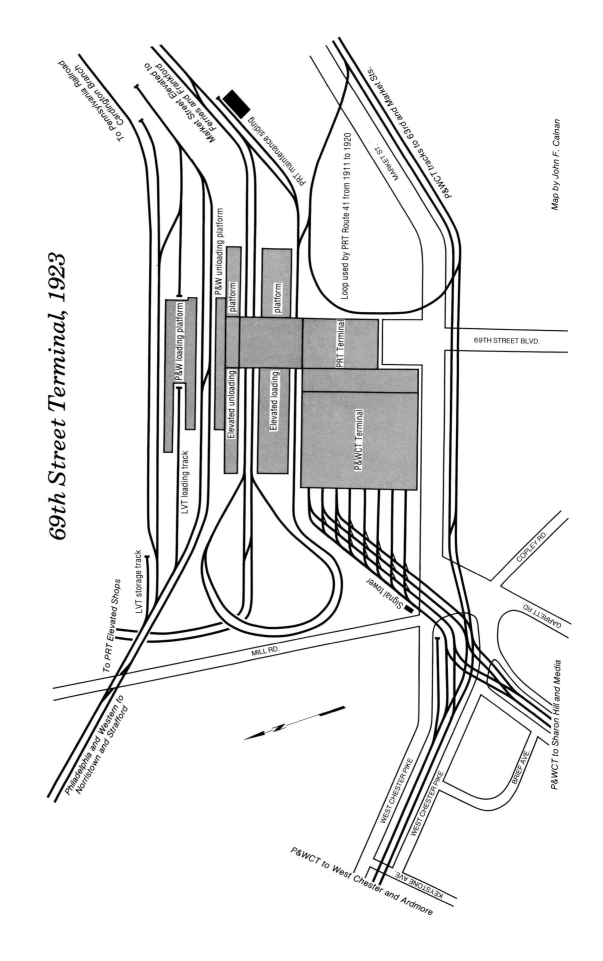

69th Street Terminal, 1923

To Pennsylvania Railroad
Cardington Branch

Market Street Elevated to
Ferries and Frankford

PRT maintenance siding

P&W unloading platform

platform

platform

P&W loading platform

Elevated unloading

Elevated loading

PRT Terminal

P&WCT Terminal

LVT loading track

To PRT Elevated Shops

LVT storage track

Philadelphia and Western to
Norristown and Strafford

MILL RD.

Signal tower

WEST CHESTER PIKE

WEST CHESTER PIKE

KEYSTONE AVE.

BRIEF AVE.

P&WCT to West Chester and Ardmore

P&WCT to Sharon Hill and Media

GARRETT RD.

COPLEY RD.

69TH STREET BLVD.

Loop used by PRT Route 41 from 1911 to 1920

MARKET ST.

P&WCT tracks to 63rd and Market Sts.

Map by John F. Calnan

and on the west was the throat of the terminal with all of its tracks and switches.

Taylor attempted to build south into West Chester Pike. He had realized as early as 1916 that the terminal would have to be expanded, and had bought some land from realtor John McClatchy. In 1922, West Chester Pike was moved south about 50 feet and the terminal was extended into the area which the road had previously occupied.

This gave the terminal three more stub-end loading tracks in addition to the original five. The expanded terminal was opened September 18, 1923. Almost immediately, stores began to be constructed on the south side of West Chester Pike. The switches leading into the terminal were rearranged so that the four northernmost tracks could be used for West Chester and Ardmore cars without conflicting with Media or Sharon Hill cars. This simplified design essentially permitted completely separate operation of the two pairs of lines, with no overlapping or conflicting movements. This resulted in increased track capacity, and made the terminal much easier to operate. The terminal expansion cost $85,000 and the new signal tower cost $52,000.

By 1922 the increase in business had required additional double-track for the Media division as far as Aronimink. The next year another section between Scenic Road and Woodland Avenue in Springfield was double-tracked. The Sharon Hill division had already been double-tracked as far as Broad Street in the Borough of Collingdale, and the Ardmore division had been double-tracked to County Line. Double-track on the West Chester division was extended from Manoa Road to Westgate Hills in 1921.

Short-turn cars began running to Aronimink in 1922 as traffic on the Media division increased. The following year, 15-minute service all day long was instituted to Media, and the short-turn trips were extended to Woodland Avenue in Springfield. Llanerch rush-hour trips also began running in 1923 to handle the crowds.

The traction company operated special "real estate excursions" on Sundays during the 1920s to lure city dwellers to buy homes in the Springfield area. This group is posed at Springfield Road Station. PST

South Ardmore was one of four small towns along the Ardmore Division between Llanerch and Ardmore. A center-door car bound for 69th Street passes through South Ardmore in the mid-1920s. The traction company installed hundreds of cast iron warning signs like the one at the right along its four rail lines. Collection of Harry P. Albrecht

No. 57 heads west on West Chester Pike at Township Line Road in 1926. PST

Income, Dividends Go Up

The traction company's finances naturally rose right along with its passenger business. The company's first dividend was paid in 1905, and for 28 years afterward—until the Depression—dividends were paid every year. Between 1905 and 1909, they amounted to only about three percent a year. They increased to four percent in 1910 and five percent in 1912. This meant that in 1912, for the first time, the dividends were equal to the amount that Eastern Securities had to pay on its stock trust certificates. For nine years, Taylor and the other owners of Eastern Securities had to put up their own funds to meet the trust certificate payments.

Dividends went up to six percent in 1914 and stayed there for many years. By 1922, the traction company was producing a 12 percent net profit.

Gross revenue rose from $146,000 in 1903 to $367,000 in 1912; $830,000 in 1919; $936,000 in 1922; and $1,639,000 in 1928.

The five cents per zone fare which had been in effect since the trolleys began running in 1895 was increased to six cents on December 3, 1918. Fares went from six to seven cents on February 27, 1924, with tickets sold at the rate of six and a quarter cents each.

"In making this moderate increase of one-quarter of a cent to the regular rider, we believe we are serving the best interests of our patrons, as this will enable us to continue to give them our high-class service and still the rates of fare charged by the traction company will be below the rates charged by any other equally equipped and operated interurban line in this section," explained a notice posted at stations.

It turned out that this increase did not produce enough additional revenue, however, and six months later fares went to eight cents, with tickets at seven and a half cents each. The fares rose to 10 cents per zone on July 20, 1927.

The Ardmore and Sharon Hill divisions were each a single zone. The Media division was two zones. The West Chester division was originally five zones, but was raised to six on September 27, 1909. The number of zones was reduced back to five on July 20, 1927.

The prosperity and rapid growth of the traction company in the early 1920s was seriously threatened by the sudden development of the motor bus.

Taylor didn't like buses—at least not in their then primitive state—but the traction company was forced into the bus business to prevent competition that could have ruined its four trolley lines. Unregulated bus routes did destroy many other suburban and interurban lines across the country during the 1920s.

The first form of rubber-tired competition came from the jitneys that swarmed throughout Delaware County by the hundreds about the time Taylor was building the Media trolley line. It must have seemed to the trolley companies in the area that everyone who owned an automobile spent his free time cruising along the rail routes picking up passengers at five cents a head.

This mildly lucrative form of moonlighting was becoming particularly popular between Lansdowne and 69th Street Terminal until both Upper Darby Township and the Borough of Lansdowne passed ordinances in 1915 requiring jitney operators to obtain licenses.

This quickly squelched the jitney drivers, and only a few of them applied for licenses. Then the Pennsylvania Public Service Commission also prohibited unlicensed jitneys, acting on the pleas of dozens of trolley companies whose profits were being damaged by the "hit-and-run" tactics of the jitneys.

The first of the regulated jitney operators around the 69th Street area was John M. Drew, who on November 19, 1918, received permission from the Public Service Commission to operate a five-passenger Ford touring car from the terminal to Lansdowne and Darby.

Drew and a friend named Louis Lind immediately formed the John Drew Auto Bus Lines. The two men raised $2,465 for the down payment on two truck chassis equipped with bus bodies, and with these vehicles they began service on February 17, 1919.

A few years later, Taylor explained his initial feelings about buses: "In the early stages of the development of the passenger motor bus, it was not apparent that this vehicle would be developed to its present state of efficiency which renders it a most serious and dangerous competitor of rail transportation. It was then comparatively uneconomical, unreliable and unsafe in operation, resulting in frequent breakdowns, especially under heavy snow and ice conditions."

Following the Drew line was Blue Bus Line in 1921. Blue Bus was formed by Adelbert H. Kay to run from 63rd and Market Streets to East Lansdowne via 69th Street Terminal. It lasted only a year. Possibly its rapid demise was due to the fact that year-round service was offered by open sightseeing buses, which must have been rather breezy in the winter.

Thomas B. Lytle asked for and received the Blue Bus franchise in mid-1922, and he began service under the name of Red Star Bus Lines (changed in 1926 to Red Star Lines) using two bus bodies mounted on truck frames. The following year he extended the route from East

Aronimink Transportation's first three buses were built in 1923 by White. Solid rubber tires and a primitive suspension system made these vehicles very rough riding, and they were replaced by more comfortable models by 1930. PST

Fageol Safety Coaches made up the second bus purchase in 1926. They were a considerable improvement over the 1923 vehicles. PST

Lansdowne to Lansdowne, and in 1924 a second route was created to serve Yeadon and part of southwest Philadelphia.

Neither the Drew nor the Red Star operations bothered the traction company, and Taylor did nothing to attempt to block either bus company. But he did successfully fight a proposal in 1922 for a bus route between Media and Newtown Square, which he felt would be competitive with his trolley lines.

That same year, a realtor who was trying to develop a section of Drexel Hill applied for a license to run a bus line on State Road and West Chester Pike to the terminal.

Meeting the Bus Threat

There were reports of other bus routes that might be established to compete with the trolleys, so Taylor decided to meet the threats head-on. By the end of 1922 the traction company had filed papers for a bus subsidiary called Aronimink Transportation Company.

The new company was officially incorporated April 4, 1923, and on December 1 Route A began operating between the terminal and Aronimink via State Road. Its entire fleet consisted of three White buses, with two of them maintaining half-hour frequency and one as a spare.

A would-be bus operator called the Delaware County Transportation Company sought permission in 1924 to run from Darby to Aldan and Springfield. The next year it asked for a line from Darby to Media.

Taylor felt this would have directly competed with the Media trolley line, so Aronimink Transportation asked for permission to extend Route A to Media along the same route the Delaware County Transportation Company was seeking. The permission was granted, and Route A buses began running to Media on May 7, 1926.

Five other applications for competitive bus lines were also filed with the Public Service Commission in 1925.

Montgomery Bus Company, a man named Vincent Mariani and Philadelphia Rural Transit Company (the bus subsidiary of Philadelphia Rapid Transit Company) all wanted to run lines from 69th Street to Ardmore.

Montgomery Bus also planned a route from Ardmore to Bon Air, which would have paralleled the Ardmore trolley line for much of the distance.

The fifth line was sought by Paul F. Stanley, who proposed to run buses on a short route connecting the Brookline station of the Ardmore trolley line with the Beechwood-Brookline station of the Philadelphia and Western Railway. And there were reports that Red Star Lines wanted to extend its Lansdowne route into part of Drexel Hill served by the Sharon Hill trolleys.

Taylor's first impulse was merely to fight these lines and attempt to block them. He had no desire to get into the bus business on a large scale because he didn't think it would be profitable then. But at the same time, if any of these other bus companies got their requested routes they would drain passengers from Taylor's trolleys.

By 1925, Taylor had reluctantly decided that Aronimink Transportation would have to fight would-be competitors by offering to provide bus service over the same routes proposed by the others. In testimony before the Public Service Commission, Taylor said he was seeking "to defend my company against an invasion of its territory and earnings which would destroy its credit as well as its ability to continue its present constructive policy."

"If certificates of public convenience are issued enabling motor bus lines to cruise on highways through districts which it has taken existing transportation lines decades to develop and to thus prey upon traffic which legitimately belongs to existing street railways, the electric railway industry would be destroyed," Taylor declared.

He promised the Public Service Commission that Aronimink Transportation would "provide motor bus lines in any portion of its territory where they are required for public service and will, within a reasonable time, yield a reasonable return upon the capital invested."

To ward off Red Star Lines, Aronimink Transportation filed a plan to run from the terminal to Abbey Terrace in Drexel Hill via Lansdowne. Service began on Route B on April 19, 1926, with 29-passenger Fageol

The traction company's first piece of non-rail work equipment was built by White Motor Company and arrived about 1920. Notice the trolley bell on the roof and the trolley-type marker lights. PST

buses. The Fageol "Safety Coaches" were an immense improvement over
the initial three White buses.

Stanley's application to run buses between the two rail stations in the
newly developed Brookline area seemed harmless enough, but Taylor was
afraid Stanley might eventually sell out to Montgomery Bus, which operated along Lancaster Pike on the Main Line. To meet this possible threat,
Aronimink Transportation asked for permission to run Route C from
69th Street to the Brookline trolley station, with a branch serving the
Parkview area along West Chester Pike. Service began on May 12, 1926.

To counter the very serious threat by the three companies that wanted
to run to Ardmore, Aronimink filed an application to operate buses
between the terminal and Ardmore. The Public Service Commission
agreed, and service on Route D began October 4. Two buses initially
provided service every half hour, but there were so few riders that the
schedule was soon cut to every hour using only one bus.

The application of Montgomery Bus to run from Ardmore to Bon Air
was countered by Aronimink Transportation's request for the same
route. Again Aronimink won, and hourly service using one bus began
May 2, 1927. This became Route E. For the first few years not enough
passengers were carried to even pay the driver's salary.

Aronimink Transportation also obtained the right on July 17, 1926, to
run local charter service.

It was obvious by this time that the Public Service Commission was
giving preference to Aronimink on any bus routes that would compete
with the traction company. But Taylor wanted a definite statement of
policy from the commission declaring that electric railways would get
preference in establishing bus routes in their territory.

In 1926 the commission agreed to this and made it official policy.

"Upon several occasions individuals have made application for short
bus routes in the territory [served by the traction company]," said the
commission. "The commission has been convinced that such applications
do not meet the requirements of the public. The various terminal points
under such applications do not afford proper traffic connections with
existing transportation facilities, and would serve only to create a dis-
connected assortment of routes operated without proper financial re-
sponsibility and without coordination in the service to the public."

The commission added that the traction company and PRT "should be
the principal agencies to meet the requirements of this rapidly growing
section for transportation service."

This was a significant pronouncement as far as the traction company
was concerned. It meant there would be no more mad scramble to ward
off outside threats to the trolley lines, and a sensible, coordinated system
of bus routes could be planned.

To service the increasing number of bus routes, Aronimink Transportation added 15 Fageol buses to its original three Whites in 1926. More
buses were added in each of the next three years.

Additional land was purchased on the west side of the original carbarn
in Llanerch in 1926, and the approach tracks to the 1907 carbarn were
removed from inside the old barn and placed on the new land. The old
carbarn was then turned into a bus garage and repair shop. The same
year a narrow strip of land was purchased along the side of 69th Street
Terminal, and buses used it as their loading and unloading area.

Taylor was correct in his initial belief that buses would not be profitable in the early 1920s. For 1924, the first full year of operation, Aronimink Transportation took in $24,000. This increased to nearly $138,000

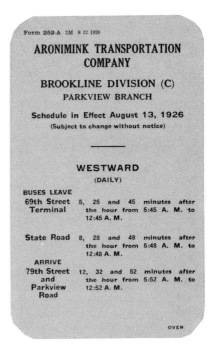

Small timecards were issued for each
of the bus routes. This 1926 card for
Route C showed 20-minute service to
Parkview and Brookline. Collection of
Ronald DeGraw

in 1926 and nearly $384,000 in 1928, which was the first year that income matched expenses.

Taylor next proposed a route from 69th Street to Oakview, a small settlement on the Sharon Hill trolley line not far from the area served by Route B. Service on the Oakview line—Route F—began on July 11, 1927, and it was later rerouted to also serve Stonehurst Hills.

Route G became the second bus line that did not run to the terminal. This was a short feeder line from the Woodland Avenue trolley station in Springfield to the Borough of Morton, and it began operating on March 15, 1928. A joint ticket between Morton and 69th Street on Route G buses and Media trolleys was 15 cents. In 1929 free transfers were issued for the first time between trolley and bus lines.

Next came a long cross-country route between Darby and Ardmore via Llanerch. This provided connections with all four trolley lines and several bus lines, and it meant that passengers could transfer from one route to another without having to enter the terminal. This was Route H, and service began on May 28, 1928.

Fares charged by Aronimink Transportation were originally the same as those on the rail lines, but because of the heavy losses the bus rates were increased to 10 cents in 1925, two years before the trolley fares reached that point.

In an attempt to attract more riders—or at least not to lose the ones it had to autos—the traction company in 1925 bought 10 more cars—Nos.

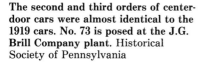

The second and third orders of center-door cars were almost identical to the 1919 cars. No. 73 is posed at the J.G. Brill Company plant. Historical Society of Pennsylvania

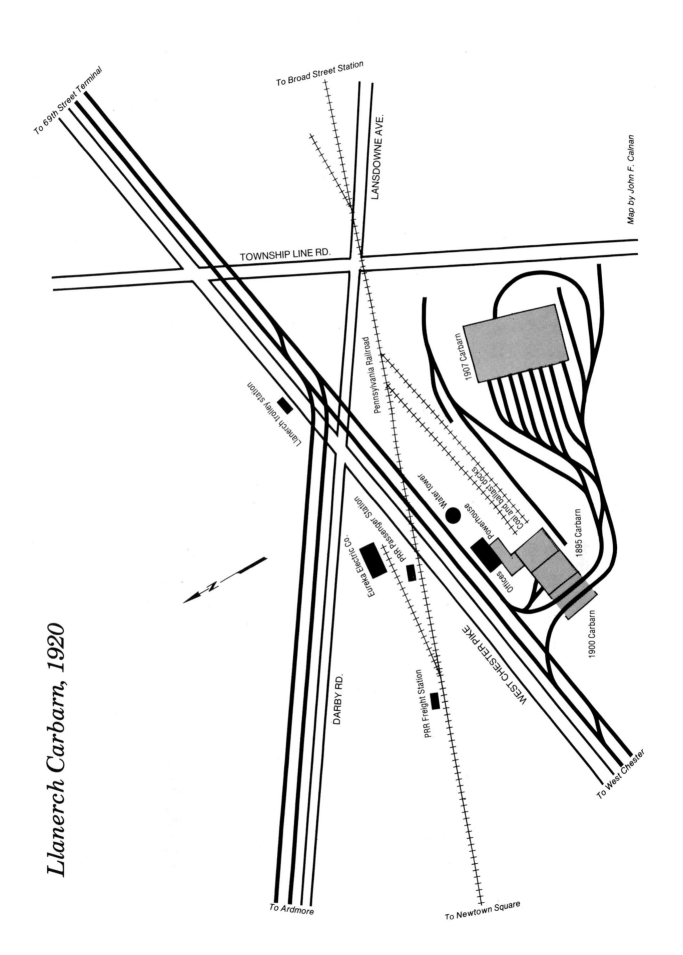

Llanerch Carbarn, 1920

Map by John F. Calnan

55–64—nearly identical to the 10 center-door cars which had been purchased in 1919. They cost $18,600 each. The following year 12 more of the same cars were bought, Nos. 65–76.

When the center-door cars were first acquired in 1919, they were a logical purchase. By the mid-1920s, however, many trolley companies across the country were changing to one-man operation in an attempt to save money. The center-door cars, though, locked Red Arrow into two-man operation, since the cars could not be properly operated without conductors. Some of the center-door cars continued in regular service through the mid-1960s, always with a motorman and conductor. The traction company later attempted to operate the center-door cars principally in two-car trains, requiring two conductors but only one motorman.

New high-speed trucks were purchased for Nos. 40–44, and the relocation of passing sidings on the West Chester division permitted a reduction in running time to West Chester from 72 to 57 minutes effective August 22, 1927.

During a hearing before the Public Service Commission in 1927, Dr. Thomas Conway, Jr., who later became president of the Philadelphia and

No. 68 was three years old when it was photographed at Llanerch in 1930. PST

Western, gave his opinion of the condition of the traction company: "This property has for a great many years been one of the best of its type in the United States. I should rank it among the first 20, probably, from the standpoint of physical condition. It is unusually good, and is one of the best-maintained properties in Pennsylvania.

"The greatest complaint I have heard, and the greatest detriment the traction company has, is the very poor standard of service on the Philadelphia subway-elevated system. I always hear talk about the rotten service on the subway."

By the end of the 1920s, the traction company was operating three of its rail lines with 15-minute service. The West Chester division still offered service only every 30 minutes. Of the eight bus routes, two—Routes D and E—were offering only 60-minute service. Three others—Routes B, C and F—were running every 20 minutes, with 12-minute peak service. Route G ran every 15 minutes. So did Route A, but during rush hours it operated every six minutes. Route H ran every 30 minutes.

Between 1923 and 1929, Aronimink Transportation had purchased 37 buses, Nos. 1–37. The one-way bus route mileage totaled 40.5 miles in 1929. The trolley system had a total of 33.9 main track miles, together with 11.6 miles of second main track and 6.2 miles of sidings and carbarn trackage, for a total of 51.7 miles.

Most of the Ardmore and Sharon Hill lines had been double-tracked, as had much of the Media line. The West Chester division would remain primarily single-track until its abandonment 25 years later.

The traction company ended the 1920s in fine condition, both physically and financially. Taylor had just given himself a salary raise to $10,985 a year, and the future of the traction company—and indeed of much of the electric railway industry—appeared secure. The collapse of the stock market was about to change all of that.

A two-car train of center-door cars loaded on track No. 3 as buses occupied the lane outside the terminal in the late 1920s. PST

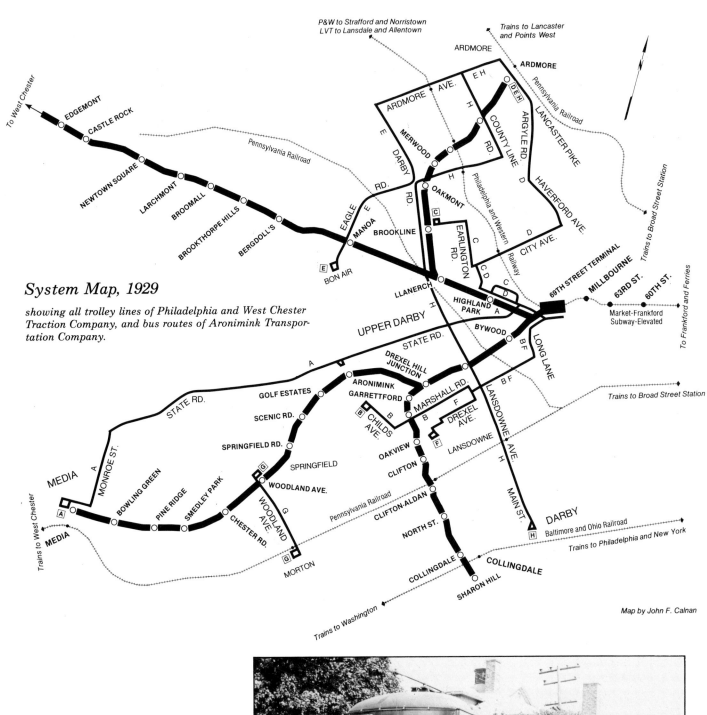

System Map, 1929

showing all trolley lines of Philadelphia and West Chester Traction Company, and bus routes of Aronimink Transportation Company.

P&W to Strafford and Norristown
LVT to Lansdale and Allentown

Trains to Lancaster and Points West

To West Chester

EDGEMONT
CASTLE ROCK
NEWTOWN SQUARE
LARCHMONT
BROOMALL
BROOKTHORPE HILLS
BERGDOLL'S

Pennsylvania Railroad

ARDMORE
ARDMORE
ARDMORE AVE.
E H
H
D E H
MERWOOD
E
COUNTY LINE RD.
ARGYLE RD.
LANCASTER PIKE
Pennsylvania Railroad

DARBY RD.
EAGLE RD.
MANOA
E
OAKMONT
H
HAVERFORD AVE.
D

BON AIR
E
BROOKLINE
C
EARLINGTON RD.
C
CITY AVE.
D

Trains to Broad Street Station

LLANERCH
HIGHLAND PARK
A
C D
69TH STREET TERMINAL
MILLBOURNE
63RD ST.
60TH ST.
To Frankford and Ferries

UPPER DARBY
BYWOOD
B F
LONG LANE
Market-Frankford Subway-Elevated

STATE RD.
A
DREXEL HILL JUNCTION
MARSHALL RD.
B F
Trains to Broad Street Station

GOLF ESTATES
ARONIMINK
GARRETTFORD
B
F
LANSDOWNE AVE.

STATE RD.
SCENIC RD.
CHILDS AVE.
B
DREXEL AVE.
F
LANSDOWNE
H

MEDIA
SPRINGFIELD RD.
OAKVIEW
MAIN ST.
DARBY
H

A
MONROE ST.
BOWLING GREEN
PINE RIDGE
SMEDLEY PARK
G
WOODLAND AVE.
SPRINGFIELD
CLIFTON

Baltimore and Ohio Railroad

MEDIA
A
CHESTER RD.
WOODLAND AVE.
G
Pennsylvania Railroad
CLIFTON-ALDAN
NORTH ST.
Trains to Philadelphia and New York

Trains to West Chester

MORTON
G

COLLINGDALE
COLLINGDALE
SHARON HILL

Trains to Washington

Map by John F. Calnan

The motorman stood behind the center window in his own private cab in center-door cars. No. 67 is at Llandillo Road en route to Ardmore. Collection of Harre W. Demoro

Chapter 6

The Blizzard of 1922

SNOWSTORMS IN EASTERN PENNSYLVANIA were often severe enough to close the trolley lines for several hours or even for a day or two.

The West Chester line was particularly susceptible to snow problems because much of the line ran adjacent to open fields and up and down hills; drifting snow caused many difficulties.

When the old steam dummies were acquired by John N.M. Shimer in 1895, a steam-powered snowplow was included in the purchase. It is most unlikely that the plow ever saw much service, however, and it was derelict by the time A. Merritt Taylor took over the presidency of the Philadelphia and West Chester Traction Company in 1899. Taylor sold or scrapped the plow later that year after finding it inoperable.

In February 1899, only a month after Taylor joined the company, there was a severe blizzard. Taylor complained to his board of directors: "I found I had no appliances for removing snow, and personally supervised the work of 175 men which took an entire week."

Taylor was a man of action, however, and within the next eight months he purchased three different types of snowplows. First to arrive were a rotary plow built by Ruggles and a sweeper built by McGuire. For some reason, both were designated No. 1. Arriving later in the year was a wedge plow—No. 3—built by Brill. All three of these cars were single-truckers, and all were retired prior to World War II.

With the opening of the Ardmore line in 1902, another single-truck sweeper—No. 2—was ordered from McGuire. A third small sweeper—No. 3—arrived in 1912. Both were scrapped immediately after World War II. A double-truck rotary snowplow built by Smith and Wallace came in 1910. It became No. 1, and the smaller rotary was renumbered No. 2.

It was with these six pieces of snow-fighting equipment that the traction company faced one of the biggest blizzards ever to hit the area on January 28, 1922. An article in the *West Chester Daily Local* of Monday, January 30, 1922, described how the storm affected passengers on the West Chester trolleys:

"Three carloads of passengers, men, women and children, on the Philadelphia & West Chester Traction Company's line were hauled to this place yesterday afternoon on sleds by a rescue party sent out by the company and their friends, after having been in the cars, stuck in the snowdrifts at three different places, for nearly twenty hours.

"The Traction Company, with sweepers and shovel gangs, kept the road open on Saturday afternoon until about 5 o'clock, when the snow proved victorious, and three cars bound for West Chester stopped short and stayed there with their passengers for many hours.

"One car was stuck just east of Milltown, another near Street Road station, and the other further down the line. The wires were soon busy, as it was seen that the cars could not be moved further Saturday night, and word was sent to West Chester police headquarters and other places; also to the trolley officials.

"Early Saturday evening a rescue party started from West Chester, but was unable to reach Milltown and had to give up the undertaking, and it was not until 5 o'clock yesterday afternoon that the last of the

The traction company's powerful double-truck rotary snowplow paused somewhere on the West Chester line during the blizzard of 1922. PST

No snowstorm was too deep for the big rotary. Here it is in action during the 1922 storm, spraying snow in all directions. PST

marooned passengers reached West Chester on the big sleds sent out from here by the officials and friends.

"Most of the people remained on the cars all night. Some food was obtained at Capt. Charles W. Manley's place for one carload, and for the other passengers milk and sandwiches were obtained at the Delchester Farms. The supply was limited, however, owing to the trouble of transportation.

"The passengers generally, many being women, accepted the inevitable

The single-track trolley line to West Chester has been cleared of snow during the blizzard of 1922, but West Chester Pike—on the right—still lies buried under several feet of snow. PST

The double-truck rotary was built in 1910 and proved a godsend during the terrible January 1922 storm. It was never again needed, and was finally scrapped in 1940. This photo was taken two years before scrapping. E. Everett Edwards

and sat down to await developments. It was seen that they were in for an all night stay. On Sunday morning, most of the parties were able to get to farmhouses and were made comfortable. Some, however, stayed in the cars, hoping for help. It came to all later in the day; the story of the rescue party sounds like an Arctic exploration tale.

"After it was found, late Saturday evening, that the stranded cars could not be reached, preparations were made to start early Sunday morning for the cars. The trolley company gave directions to the police officials and others here to obtain transportation and go get the passengers, and several contractors and others with horses and sleds were employed. There were several volunteers, friends of the folks in the snowbound cars, willing to help. Councilman Rambo offered the borough horses, and Street Commissioner Reagan led a half dozen of the big horses, riding bareback with his impromptu cavalcade. These went ahead to 'blaze' the way. It was found necessary after the pilots had reached the Fair Grounds to take to the fields, as the roadways were drifted full. From there on to the Street Road, the party took down rail fences, cut wire fences and zig-zagged through bars and gates and lanes. It was hard and cold work. The sled party followed the horsemen with some difficulty.

"The first party to be reached were those at Milltown, and a sled load

Sweeper No. 4 was built by McGuire-Cummings in 1922, and is one of two sweepers still active on the Media and Sharon Hill lines. PST

The single-truck rotary plow arrived in 1899 and remained on the property until the mid-1950s. This view was taken at Llanerch in 1952. Robert L. Long

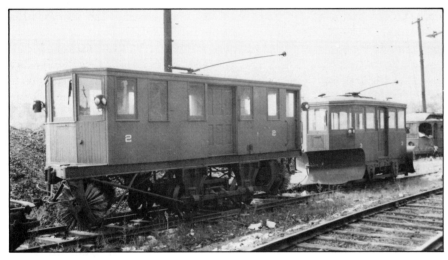

A single-truck sweeper and the single-truck wedge plow were stored at the Llanerch carbarn in 1947. North Jersey Chapter, NRHS

of tired, sleepy, hungry passengers were hauled into West Chester over the fields. They got in about 2 p.m. The remainder of the rescuers kept on down the road, and later in the afternoon reached the Delchester Farms, where they found most of the passengers at a farm house. It was there that some movie picture films could have been taken, as women as well as men were helped on horses and rode bareback to the sleds up the road. But that was no time for ceremony or squeamishness, and so they rode astride. The last sled load arrived in West Chester about 5 o'clock. It was a tired party, but happy withal, and very grateful, too, for the men who went out in the rescue party had a hard job. They were tired and cold, also hungry. The borough horses were hitched on in front of the other horses, harness having been commandeered from several barns.

"There were numerous interesting stories told by those who were marooned. There were many incidents, some thrills, and numerous spills. The courage and endurance of some of the women was creditable, and while it was a tiresome wait, there was considerable merriment on board the cars. Fortunately, so far as learned, there were no injuries, but some no doubt will suffer from colds."

Despite severe drifts that closed parts of West Chester Pike for many days during this storm, the trolley line was crippled for only two days. The town of West Chester was shut off from the rest of the world for nearly a week except for the single-track trolley line. The hero of the hour was the double-truck rotary snow plow, which managed to eliminate even the deepest drifts. This was the last time the big rotary was needed, although it was kept around for about 18 years longer before being scrapped.

The traction company was apparently not pleased with the performance of the single-truck sweepers during the 1922 blizzard, because immediately afterward it ordered a new double-truck sweeper from McGuire-Cummings. The sweeper cost $4,000 and became No. 4.

One more double-truck sweeper—No. 5—was purchased second-hand from Syracuse Railways in 1940. It was built by Russell.

By the late 1940s, only the two double-truck sweepers—Nos. 4 and 5— remained in service, and they are still operating in the 1980s as the only snow-fighting equipment for the Media and Sharon Hill lines.

No. 5 pauses just outside 69th Street Terminal as No. 82, laden with icicles, attempts to run to Ardmore. William Crawford

Chapter 7

Trolleys Carry the Freight

T HE TURNPIKE AND THE TROLLEY LINE had both been built to serve a rural population made up largely of farmers, so it was only natural that milk and freight services were operated.

First of the non-passenger services, however, was mail, but it didn't come about because the traction company dreamed of great profits.

Even before the last of the steam dummies stopped chugging between 63rd Street and Llanerch, there were rumblings of a strike by the company's motormen and conductors unless their wages were increased to the same as the Philadelphia trolley lines paid. John Shimer, aware that it would probably be only a few more weeks before he got court permission to run his electric cars over the Pennsylvania Railroad crossing at Llanerch, wasn't about to let a strike ruin his dream.

So off he went to Washington, and with his glib tongue managed to convince the Post Office Department to award him a mail contract effective June 1, 1896. Previously the mail had been carried by stage coaches.

Shimer hustled back to Llanerch and had the words "U.S. Mail" painted in large gold letters on the front and back of all his trolleys, confident that his employees wouldn't dare strike a company that had a government mail contract. He was correct.

Mail was carried on regularly scheduled passenger cars. The Newtown Square Post Office got its mail by trolley until the line was abandoned in 1954.

The Pennsylvania Railroad monopolized the West Chester and Ardmore post offices, but the trolleys carried the mail between Media and 69th Street and between West Chester and Edgemont, a profitable arrangement that lasted until June 30, 1963.

Farmers all along the turnpike had to cart their milk into the city every day, a slow and expensive process which consumed nearly a full day. In January 1897, only eight months after through trolley service had begun, Shimer inaugurated a daily milk run. Business was light at first, and a little four-wheel car converted from a steam dummy was sufficient to handle the traffic.

This car was No. 1, an obvious conflict of numbering with the existing passenger cars and with the company's only work car. But this apparently didn't bother the company, because throughout its history there would be a total of nine cars designated as No. 1.

Business boomed quickly, and more than a million quarts of milk were handled during the first year. Farmers built little wooden platforms next to the trolley line level with the floor of the milk car. Early each morning except Sundays the trolley stopped at the platforms and its crew lifted the big containers of milk into the car.

The trolley then ran to 63rd and Market Streets, where the company built a siding and platform on a vacant lot on the southwest corner. Horse-drawn wagons from the city's biggest milk companies waited for the arrival of the trolley, and the milk was quickly transferred to the wagons. Next morning on its way out the trolley dropped off all the empty milk cans at the farmers' platforms.

A. Merritt Taylor expanded the milk business considerably, pushing it out to Milltown in the summer of 1899 and ultimately as far as Cottage Hill, which was at the eastern borough limits of West Chester, by 1916. The milk car left Cottage Hill at 7:03 a.m. each morning during the summer, arriving at 9:12 a.m. at 63rd Street. It ran an hour later during the winter.

The milk runs were always confined to the West Chester division, which ran past many farms. Sidings were installed at Newtown Square and Castle Rock, two of the busiest milk pickup points.

Business grew so fast that the little four-wheel car was scrapped after only two years in favor of a double-truck car—also No. 1—built by Jackson and Sharp in 1899.

No. 06, a big fast car built by the Jewett Car Company, arrived in 1909 to replace the second No. 1. In 1911, No. 06 received a primitive cooling system in an attempt to prevent the milk from spoiling on hot days. An ice box was built into one end of the car, and a large fan blowing over the ice was supposed to circulate the cool air.

Milk cans had to have tickets or tags, which were sold in 20- and 40-quart denominations. A 20-quart shipment cost seven and a half cents in 1915, and was raised to nine cents by 1918.

The 63rd Street milk and freight station was a busy place after the milk trolley arrived every morning except Sunday. PST

Shipping the milk in bottles instead of in cans cost more, and bottled cream cost about twice as much as canned milk.

"The company will not be responsible for rejected milk or cream, nor for loss of or injury to cans, boxes or bottles," the traction company told its customers. "Shipper must load cans or cases on cars when required to do so, and consignees are expected to meet car on arrival at destination."

Annual receipts for milk rose to $17,000 by 1908, but 10 years later they had been cut almost in half, partly because of the increasing growth of the motor truck. After the extension of service to Cottage Hill in 1916 and an increase in rates, milk revenue climbed back to almost $15,000 in 1922.

Suddenly the bottom dropped out of the milk business when Supplee-Wills-Jones Dairy Company—the traction company's chief customer at 63rd Street—decided to send its own trucks along West Chester Pike beginning October 1, 1924.

Overnight the milk trolley died. Shipments immediately dropped to about 30 cans a day, less than one-quarter of what had previously been carried.

The milk business quickly became a liability instead of a profit-maker, and on January 27, 1925, No. 06 made its last trip. The car was sold later that year.

A once-lively freight business was also discontinued the same day, it, too, having fallen victim to highway competition.

It was not unusual for trolley companies to carry light freight, and many of them made a substantial profit on it. The Pennsylvania legislature passed a law in 1907 permitting trolley companies to carry

A simple open platform served as the milk transfer point. The 63rd Street station of the Market Street Elevated loomed overhead. PST

freight, and Taylor decided to try his hand at it beginning in the spring of 1911.

This was no quick decision, because it required the construction of several freight houses and the purchase of a new express car. Three existing work cars were also used for freight service, and in 1918 a refrigerated express car was purchased to carry vegetables and other foodstuffs.

A three-track freight terminal was built where the milk cars unloaded at 63rd and Market Streets, almost directly under the 63rd Street station of the Market Street Elevated. One of the tracks was used for the traction company's milk cars. The freight trolleys used an adjacent track built next to a freight house, and Philadelphia Rapid Transit Company freight trolleys used the third track on the other side of the freight house, permitting goods to be transferred across a platform between the cars of the two companies.

PRT already operated a big freight station at Front and Market Streets, adjacent to the city's produce and waterfront district. A joint

No. 1 was the second milk car, acquired by the traction company in 1899. PST

A larger car, No. 06, was acquired in 1909 for the milk business. It had a primitive refrigeration system. PST

agreement was drawn up between the two companies to ship merchandise from downtown Philadelphia to suburban destinations.

Freight stations with sidings were built at Clifton and Ardmore. Agents were on duty at these two stations and at Llanerch and Newtown Square. In 1914 a store at the corner of West Chester Pike and Garrett Road became the Upper Darby freight station.

Non-agent delivery points were established at Broomall, Edgemont, Manoa, Milltown and Street Road, near the Ridley Creek powerhouse. Drexel Hill was added as a non-agent station in 1916.

West Chester also had an agent at an old house on Gay Street which was converted into a freight station.

There were originally four scheduled freight runs each day, although extra runs were made when necessary. One car ran from 63rd Street to West Chester, back to 63rd Street, out to West Chester again, then terminated at Llanerch. The other car ran from 63rd Street to Clifton, over to Ardmore, back to 63rd Street, then to Clifton and Ardmore again, ending at Llanerch.

This provided morning and afternoon deliveries from Philadelphia, and the schedules of the two trolley companies were so well coordinated that freight was delivered within a few hours after it left Front and Market Streets. A West Chester businessman could telephone an order for merchandise to a Philadelphia distributor early in the morning and receive delivery by midafternoon.

The traction company did not attempt to haul freight between Clifton and Sharon Hill or between Drexel Hill and Media, because these areas were already being served by PRT freight trolleys.

Receipts from the freight service were split evenly between the two companies, except that for shipments west of Newtown Square the traction company got two-thirds of the revenue.

Nearly all of the shipments were in a westwardly direction, and much of the business came from groceries shipped from the Dock Street market

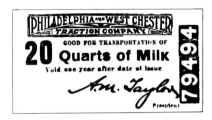

A major milk receiving point was located near Castle Rock, complete with a siding and high-level platforms. Farmers have gathered early on a warm morning to await the milk car. Wet blankets help to keep the milk cans cool. Chester County Historical Society

(which was only a few blocks from Front and Market Streets) to stores and individuals.

Although Taylor was convinced the freight experiment would work, he didn't want to spend a lot of money building a separate freight house and siding in the Borough of West Chester until he was certain it would be worthwhile. The traction company and the borough drew up an agreement permitting the freight trolleys to unload right in the middle of Gay Street at Walnut Street, a short distance east of the end of the line, until April 1, 1912.

A Fight Over Freight

Early in 1912, after six months of operation, the freight service still wasn't showing a profit. But Taylor decided to proceed with building an off-street freight station in West Chester, and paid $6,500 for a vacant lot on Walnut Street north of Gay Street, behind the post office. Installing the siding and paving 24 inches on the outside of the rails would have brought the total cost to $9,000.

Borough council then decided it wanted the traction company to pave the full block of Walnut Street, from curb to curb, at an additional cost of $4,500. The company balked and a big fight loomed. Council gave Taylor an ultimatum: Pave the street or keep your freight trolleys out of our town. The deadline was April 1.

Taylor took his grievance to the public, and on March 28, 1912, a half-page advertisement in the *West Chester Daily Local*, signed by Taylor, declared: "The West Chester merchants have been ordering large shipments of perishable vegetables, etc., from the Dock Street market. These goods have been shipped at high speed directly to the merchants' stores in West Chester. They will now be compelled to go back to the old system of shipping by express at increased rates, or by having the goods hauled from the Dock Street market to the Pennsylvania Railroad Company's West Philadelphia Freight Station at added expense for shipment thence by P.R.R. freight."

EXPRESS SERVICE

AT

FREIGHT RATES

On and after Tuesday, August 1, 1911, Express Freight Service will be established on the lines of this Company, with provision for collection and delivery of freight by the Philadelphia Rapid Transit Company, at Station, Front and Market Streets, Philadelphia.

The following freight stations will be established on August 1st, 1911:

SIXTY-THIRD & MARKET STS., PHILA.
UPPER DARBY
LLANERCH
MANOA
NEWTOWN SQUARE
WEST CHESTER

ARDMORE   CLIFTON HEIGHTS

Additional STATIONS will be established to meet traffic requirements.

FOR FURTHER INFORMATION, RATES, Etc.,
APPLY TO

PHILADELPHIA & WEST CHESTER TRACTION COMPANY
SIXTY-NINTH STREET TERMINAL

UPPER DARBY P. O., PENNA.

A few months after trolley freight service began in 1911, the traction company proudly lined up its entire fleet of freight cars in front of the Llanerch carbarn. From right to left are Nos. 07 and 06, built by Jewett in 1909; No. 01, Jackson and Sharp, 1899; No. 02, reportedly built by the traction company from one of the single-truck open cars; and No. 04, built in 1905. Collection of John Gibb Smith, Jr.

View of the 63rd Street freight and milk terminal in 1912, with the elevated line overhead. Two PRT freight trolleys are in the siding on the right side of the freight house. The other three cars belong to the traction company. PST

63rd Street from under the elevated, looking westward. The freight terminal is to the left and Millbourne Mills is on the right. PST

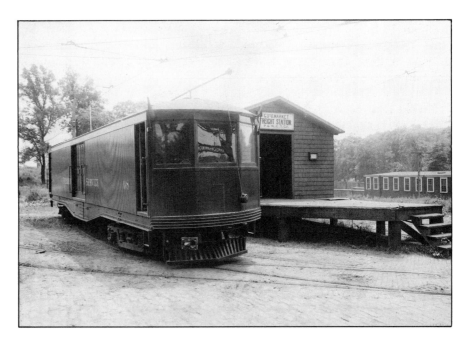

No. 08 was a refrigerated car built by Brill in 1918. It was used chiefly to carry fresh produce to merchants along the traction company's lines. The car was sold in 1925 to Sand Springs Railway. PST

Notices went up at the Gay Street freight house that service would end March 30—and it did.

A friend of Taylor's, Thomas W. Marshall, president of the National Bank of Chester County, wrote to him in June: "Some parties are disposed to waste their time in giving forth 'Hot Air' and I believe the most effective method is to do nothing in the freight matter, but simply allow them a little time to cool off."

It took more than four years for the cooling off to occur, however, for it wasn't until October 24, 1916, that the company was once again invited to run its freight trolleys down Gay Street, and this time Taylor built the Walnut Street freight station on his own terms. It opened in 1918. In the interim the freight service had terminated at Milltown.

Bond's Feed Store, at the intersection of West Chester Pike and Garrett Road, acted as the traction company's Upper Darby freight agent. PST

About 10 million pounds of merchandise were carried annually in the early years. That nearly doubled in 1917 with the extension to West Chester, and receipts that year were $15,500. But by 1920 it had slipped back down to 15 million pounds.

Volume continued to decline each year, although an increase in rates and more long-distance business caused receipts to increase to $22,000 in 1920, resulting in a small profit. By that year, 62 percent of all freight was to or from West Chester, more than 15 percent was for Clifton and less than 10 percent was for Ardmore.

Three years later more than 125 West Chester businessmen or individuals were shipping by trolley freight, and the company boasted that its rates were much cheaper than those charged by Adams Express Company.

Adams charged 50 cents to ship 100 pounds of tires, toys, whiskey, saddlery or tobacco from West Chester to Philadelphia via the Pennsylvania Railroad. The traction company charged 15 cents.

Adams charged the same rate for sugar and salt, but it could be shipped on the trolleys for nine cents. Other traction company rates were comparably lower.

The highest price charged was for bananas. Adams charged $1.00 for 100 pounds and the traction company 40 cents. Next highest was "household goods," which were 22½ cents by trolley or $1.00 by train.

Motor trucks were coming of age, however, and they slowly began

The Clifton freight station is across the tracks from the passenger station. The single-track Southern Pennsylvania Traction Company's line between Angora and Media runs in the middle of Baltimore Pike in the foreground. The sign on the station lists connecting lines to Norristown, Allentown, Coatesville, Kennett Square and other locations. PST

No. 01 has just unloaded a platform full of goods at the original Clifton freight station. Collection of David H. Cope

The traction company's original freight station in West Chester was a converted house on Gay Street at Walnut Street, near the end of the line. There was no siding, and trolleys simply unloaded their cargo in the middle of the town's main street. PST

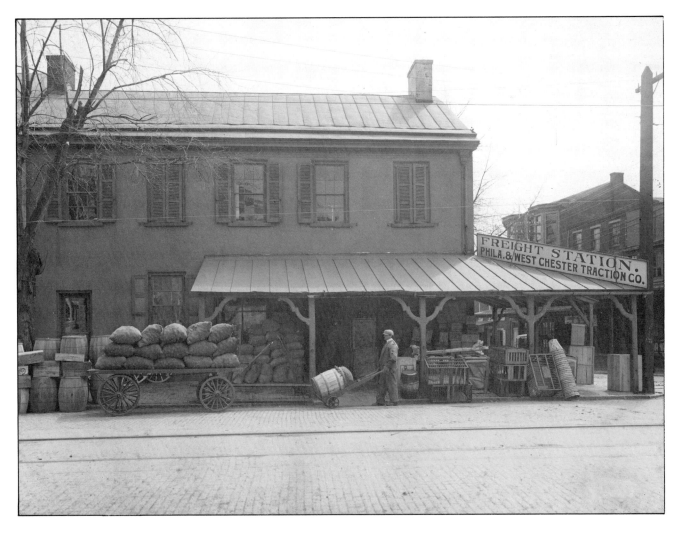

Two motorized flatcars with cabs on each end—Nos. 04 and 05—were used for both maintenance work and freight service. One of the cars is in maintenance service on the West Chester line about 1915. North Jersey Chapter, NRHS

No. 05 was a useful car for transporting hay. Wilbur P. Hall

cutting into the company's business. They cut even more deeply into the freight business of PRT, and on April 1, 1921, freight service between 63rd Street and Front and Market Streets was discontinued, leaving the suburban trolleys without a freight connection.

Complaints by the traction company and shippers convinced PRT to resume running its freight cars only three days later, but PRT declared it would get out of the business as quickly as possible.

Taylor suggested PRT set up additional freight stations in the city as a means of generating more business. PRT said no. PRT suggested it could share equally with the traction company's receipts on West Chester freight. Taylor said no, because this would create a huge freight deficit for the traction company.

PRT then suggested an organization could be formed to conduct all trolley freight service in the Philadelphia area, but, of course, nobody wanted to take on such a money-losing task.

Then again on June 1, 1922, PRT stopped running its freight cars. The traction company called on the Pennsylvania Public Service Commission to force PRT to put back its cars, but the commission said it lacked jurisdiction. Desperate, the traction company went to court and got an order compelling the commission to hear the case. But the commission again failed to act, and by this time the traction company's freight revenue had dropped 90 percent and the service was running deeply in the red.

Facing a hopeless situation, the traction company finally gave up on January 27, 1925.

Without milk and freight service, the double-track line between 63rd and Market Streets and 69th Street Terminal was virtually useless. It was being used by only one car a day, the 4:13 a.m. to West Chester.

This section of trackage had experienced an extremely colorful history. The first year it had carried steam dummies, then in 1896 little four-wheel electric cars began trundling over it from the company's 63rd and Market Streets terminal.

All West Chester, Ardmore and Clifton cars used it until 69th Street Terminal was opened in 1907. Between then and 1911 a shuttle car operated between 63rd Street and 69th Street. The trackage became part of a full route again on January 16, 1911, when PRT began running its Route 41 trolleys from Front and Market Streets to 69th and Market Streets,

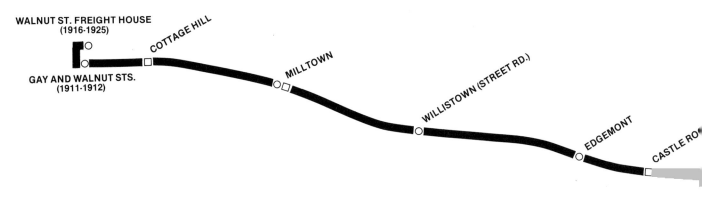

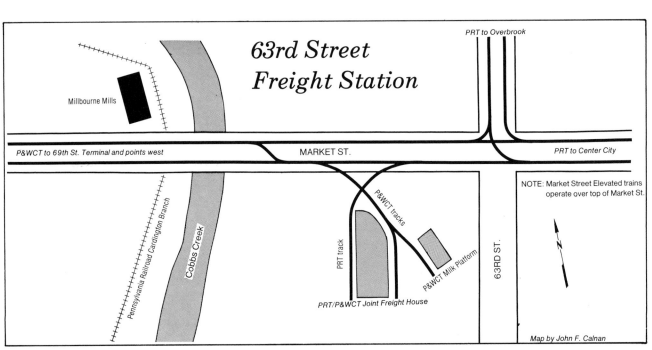

No. 07, a freight motor built in 1909, was still active in the mid-1980s as the sole work car for the Media and Sharon Hill lines. In the early 1950s, it was repainted red and cream with black and silver striping, its most handsome paint scheme. David H. Cope

Freight Service

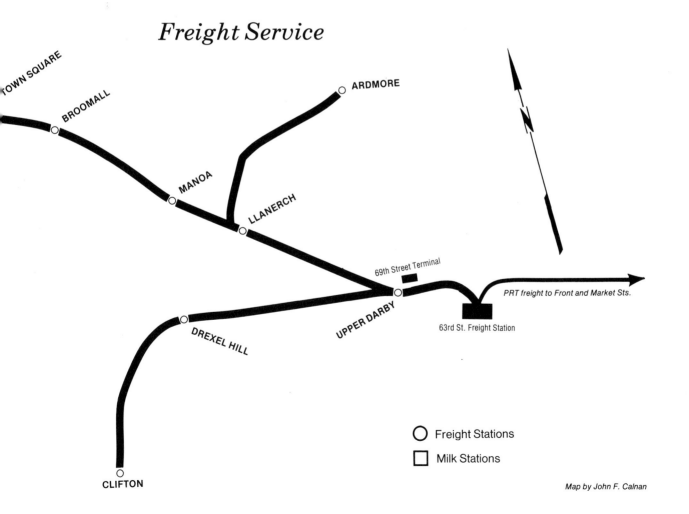

ARDMORE

TOWN SQUARE

BROOMALL

MANOA

LLANERCH

69th Street Terminal

PRT freight to Front and Market Sts.

UPPER DARBY

63rd St. Freight Station

DREXEL HILL

CLIFTON

O Freight Stations

☐ Milk Stations

Map by John F. Calnan

looping next to the entrance to PRT's portion of the terminal building.

PRT discontinued using the trackage on September 22, 1920, cutting its cars back to 63rd Street, and until 1925 it was used almost solely for freight and milk cars and for the delivery of new trolleys from the J.G. Brill plant in West Philadelphia.

PRT also occasionally used it to move trolleys to the 69th Street Elevated maintenance shops. There was a connection between the old Route 41 loop at the terminal and a loading track of the elevated at 69th Street.

With vehicular traffic increasing, the tracks were becoming a nuisance and they made it impossible to widen West Chester Pike. The last trolley ran on this section of trackage on April 5, 1926, and track removal began the next day.

Market Street is being rebuilt into a concrete highway in this 1920 view at Powell Lane in Millbourne. A PRT Route 41 trolley is traveling toward Philadelphia, a few weeks before the route was cut back to 63rd Street. After these tracks were removed in 1926, Market Street was widened. PST

Chapter 8

Battling the Great Depression, 1930–1939

WHEN THE BOTTOM FELL OUT of the stock market in October 1929, it marked the beginning of the end of the line for hundreds of electric railway routes throughout the United States.

Many of the lines ended the 1920s in weak financial and physical condition. Auto and bus competition had stolen many of their riders, and decreasing revenues had caused them to defer maintenance and the purchase of new cars. Lines in such condition fell quickly when the Depression came. Total electric railway mileage in the nation was nearly 35,000 in 1930; by 1940 it had dropped to 18,000. Even many of the lines that managed to survive the Great Depression did so tenuously, and after the boom traffic of World War II was over they, too, were abandoned, causing electric railway mileage to drop to 10,000 by 1950.

The traction company, however, was never in really serious financial condition during the entire Depression. It entered the Depression in the best physical and financial shape it had ever been in. And it remained in excellent physical condition and in satisfactory financial condition in even the darkest years of the 1930s because of the extraordinary management decisions of A. Merritt Taylor and his son, Merritt H. Taylor.

As the Depression hit, riders and revenue began to decrease rapidly. Most trolley and interurban lines reacted by reducing service, which caused more riders to desert. With revenues sinking lower and lower, the companies cut service even more and raised fares, which caused still more passengers to disappear. It was a vicious circle, made even worse by deferring all but essential maintenance. Cars which had outlived their economic usefulness were not replaced or rehabilitated because of lack of funds. The poor equipment and poor track caused running times to lengthen and the number of breakdowns to increase, making it even easier for competing buses to lure away passengers.

The traction company, however, did not follow any of the steps taken by most of the nation's electric railways. The traction company instead took bold, perhaps almost risky, action to ensure its survival. Instead of raising fares, Taylor lowered them. As ridership declined, service was not decreased. Maintenance on the physical plant continued, and new trolleys and buses were purchased.

Another important reason for the traction company's continuing financial health was the decision by Taylor in 1930 to expand the bus system. It is ironic that Aronimink Transportation Company, which Taylor originally had not even wanted to create, helped to prevent the traction company from going into bankruptcy during the early 1930s.

Aronimink Transportation nearly doubled in size in 1930 by acquiring Red Star Lines, Drew Bus Line and part of the Southern Pennsylvania

Traction Company's franchises. The purchase meant that the traction company now controlled all of the suburban bus routes operating in the 69th Street Terminal area.

The acquisitions came about because of another threat of competition. Southern Pennsylvania Traction's Baltimore Pike trolley line between Media and Angora, at the city limits at 61st Street and Baltimore Avenue, had been unprofitable for many years. As early as 1909, the company had tried to build a connection to 69th Street Terminal. Now it planned to buy the Drew Bus Line between 69th Street and Lansdowne, replace the Baltimore Pike trolleys with buses and run a through bus route from the terminal to Media and Chester via Baltimore Pike. An agreement of sale was reached with Drew in December 1929.

Taylor feared that such a move would have an adverse effect on both the Media and Sharon Hill trolley lines, so he immediately began bargaining with Southern Pennsylvania to see if he could buy both the Drew line and the Baltimore Pike trolley franchise. An agreement was reached on March 31, 1930, and on June 9 the Public Service Commission granted its approval. Aronimink Transportation paid $400,000 in cash and preferred stock for the Drew franchises and $225,000 for the Baltimore Pike franchise.

The last trolleys ran on Baltimore Pike on August 3, 1930, and the next day Aronimink Transportation began operating its buses between Angora and Media on the new Route N.

A Drew bus met an Aronimink Transportation coach in front of 69th Street Terminal in 1926. The Drew routes became Aronimink's Routes M and O. PST

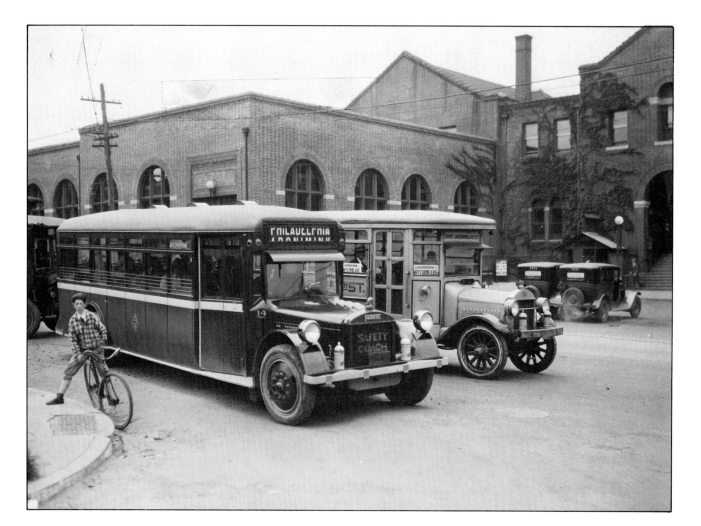

The Drew lines to Lansdowne and Darby were taken over on July 10, 1930. The Darby line became Route M and the Lansdowne line was Route O. Red Star Lines was purchased the same year for $175,000, with Aronimink taking over on October 10. Red Star's Lansdowne route was consolidated with Route F, and its Yeadon and southwest Philadelphia line became Route J on December 29.

The Red Star, Drew and Baltimore Pike routes produced revenues of $87,000 in 1931.

Aronimink Transportation also expanded in other directions. Route I was established between 69th Street Terminal and Overbrook on July 28, 1930. Route O was extended to Gladstone Manor on Baltimore Pike on April 20, 1931, and to Swarthmore on June 13, 1932. Route E was extended from Bon Air to Aronimink in 1932.

With all of these additional bus routes, Aronimink purchased 19 new buses—Nos. 38-56—in 1930. Another five—Nos. 60-64—arrived in 1933.

JOHN M. DREW
AUTO BUS TRANSIT
GOOD FOR ONE RIDE BETWEEN
BALT. AVE. AND 69th ST.
EITHER DIRECTION
Not Good Below Balt. Ave
YOU MUST DEPOSIT IN BOX ON WAY OUT
149457

The John M. Drew Auto Bus Company operated yellow Mack buses between 69th Street Terminal, Lansdowne and Darby. The routes were taken over by Aronimink Transportation in 1930. PST

Ten more—Nos. 70-79—came in 1934, and another four—Nos. 90-93—came in 1935. This brought to 79 the total number of buses which had been acquired by Aronimink Transportation since it began operating in 1923, including four used buses acquired in 1929. The buses were built by White Motor Bus Company, Fageol Bus Company, Twin Coach Company and Mack-International Truck Company. Not all 79 of the buses were in operation at any one time, however, since the life of early buses was short and several of the oldest vehicles had been scrapped or sold.

Taylor did not consider the buses operated by Drew or Red Star Lines to be satisfactory for his passengers, so he purchased only the route rights and not the vehicles. With very few exceptions throughout its history, Aronimink and its successors acquired new buses rather than used ones.

The 1932 route extensions brought the total bus network to 67 one-way route miles. No more new bus routes or extensions were created until

Merritt H. Taylor became president of
the traction company in 1932.
Collection of Merritt H. Taylor, Jr.

1936, although increasing ridership required additional buses to be purchased in 1933, 1934 and 1935.

Of all the bus routes, the most prosperous one remained the original Route A.

Ridership Plummets

The traction company almost immediately felt the effects of the Depression. Income fell by $10,000 in 1929, to $1,629,000. In 1930 it climbed back to $1,695,000 and in 1931 to $1,757,000. But these two increases were due solely to the acquisition of the Drew, Red Star and Baltimore Pike routes. During 1931 alone the number of riders on the other bus and rail lines dropped by nine percent.

As the Depression worsened, ridership went down rapidly. Gross revenue for the combined bus and rail operation fell to $1.4 million in 1932 and to $1.2 million in 1933. The sudden drop resulted in deficits for both years. In 1931 one out of every three passengers was carried on the bus lines, a ratio that stayed about the same during the entire Depression. Without those bus riders, the traction company would have been in serious financial difficulty.

Minor service cuts on the trolleys occurred in 1931, when the previous all-night service on the trolley lines was replaced by buses operating only as far as Oakmont on the Ardmore division and Aronimink on the Media division between about 1:00 a.m. and 5:00 a.m. No service ran to Sharon Hill or West Chester during these hours. This resulted in savings in electric power costs.

There were no other noticeable schedule cuts, even though many vehicles were running almost empty at times. Taylor reasoned that the most important way to survive the Depression was to keep as many passengers as possible. He therefore refused to make any substantial service reductions, a policy completely contrary to that followed by most other transit companies in the country.

Another radical step taken by Taylor was to buy new cars in the face of mounting losses and decreasing ridership. The traction company ordered five new trolleys—Nos. 77-81—at a cost of $19,500 each. They arrived in early 1932, and were placed in service on the Media division on April 17, 1932, where they had a chance to show off their rapid acceleration and high-speed capabilities. They permitted the running time to Media to be trimmed by four minutes, so that the line could be operated with four cars instead of five. These were the first lightweight, one-man, high-speed cars on the system.

Immediately after they arrived, the traction company ordered five more, Nos. 82-86, at a reduced price of $18,100 each. They went into service on the West Chester division on July 10, 1932, performing all midday service. Both groups of cars were acquired under a lease-purchase arrangement with Brill, so that the traction company did not have to immediately put up large amounts of cash for their acquisition.

The increased speed, reduced power consumption and one-man operation of the new cars resulted in annual savings of about $42,000. The new cars also permitted the remainder of the old Brill and Jewett interurbans —except Nos. 40-44—to be scrapped.

A general wage reduction for all employees of 10 percent became effective December 1, 1931. A second wage reduction of 7.4 percent occurred on December 1, 1932.

These Twin Coach buses were the most modern things on rubber wheels when this photo was taken in 1934. PST

To compound the problems facing the company, its president was forced to retire because of poor health. Taylor had suffered a stroke in the late 1920s, and his declining health finally convinced him to step down as president of the traction company on March 2, 1932. He was named chairman of the board, and his son, Merritt H. Taylor, was elected president.

Merritt Taylor was born in Merion, Pennsylvania, on August 2, 1899, the same year his father had been elected president of the struggling little country trolley line. He was graduated from St. Luke's School in Wayne, Pennsylvania, and Massachusetts Institute of Technology, where he received a degree in mechanical and electrical engineering in 1920. He served as a first lieutenant of infantry during World War I.

For nearly a year after graduation, he worked in the Thomas A. Edison Laboratories in Orange, New Jersey, then went to work for the traction company as a car cleaner on March 16, 1921. After serving briefly as a mechanic, a member of the line gang, a trolley conductor, an engineer and acting superintendent of maintenance, he was named second vice president in charge of power and maintenance on November 26, 1924, at a salary of $6,000. At the same time, he became a director of the company.

His salary was increased to $10,000 in 1928, almost as much as his father was making, and it was obvious that he would become the next president.

Only a month after he was elected president, the younger Taylor made the momentous decision to reduce fares. He slashed fares for regular riders by 25 percent.

The basic cash fare remained at 10 cents per zone, but discount tickets were sold. On April 15, books of 50 commutation tickets were offered for sale at $3.75, or seven and a half cents a ride. School tickets were introduced for the first time and were sold at the same price. The tickets were an immediate success at a time when most passengers carefully rationed every penny.

Books of 30 tickets were introduced on June 13 for $2.50, or eight and

No. 92 arrived in 1935, wearing the new "A.T. Co." logo. PST

one-third cents a ride. These appealed to persons who didn't ride frequently enough to invest in the 50-ticket books. On the same date, strips of 11 tickets for $1.00 were also offered. A further reduction in school tickets came on September 6 when they were cut to 50 for $2.50, or a nickel a ride. And a five-cent cash fare was created for children up to 12 years old.

Within a short time, nearly everybody was using tickets and saving money. Before the fare reductions, the average zone fare received was 9.6 cents. Within three years it had fallen to 8.5 cents.

Ridership and income continued to drop in 1933, but then beginning in 1934 a surprising recovery in ridership developed. By 1937 the traction company was carrying as many riders as its previous all-time high of 1931. Revenues did not recover as quickly as patronage because they had been drastically cut. But the people had come back, and the fares could always be raised again after the nation had recovered from the Depression. One more fare reduction occurred in 1937. The fare to West Chester was reduced from five zones to four, and the fare to Newtown Square, which

Nos. 77-81 under construction at the J.G. Brill Company plant in Philadelphia. Collection of Ronald DeGraw

was a two-zone ride, was cut from 20 cents to 15.

The traction company took any steps it could think of to increase ridership. Joint tickets with Chester Valley Bus Lines were introduced in 1933, providing a ride from 69th Street to Downingtown via West Chester for 60 cents and to Coatesville for 75 cents. Both types of tickets were reduced by 10 cents in 1936. Chester Valley Bus Lines was the successor to West Chester Street Railway, whose trolley lines had been abandoned.

Excursions to Robin Hood Dell, a city-owned outdoor amphitheater in Fairmount Park offering free concerts, were operated for 30 cents a round trip beginning in 1935.

A small portion of double-track on the Sharon Hill division was torn up. The double-track had gone as far as Broad Street in Collingdale; it was cut back about two blocks to North Street, near the boundary between Collingdale and Aldan. The small saving in running time was just enough to permit short-turn Aldan cars to operate more efficiently.

The Ridley Creek and Aronimink substations were automated, and power switches were installed at the junctions of Drexel Hill and Llanerch.

New Cars Pondered

Taylor considered ordering 10 more lightweight trolley cars in 1934, but couldn't raise the money. Again in 1936 negotiations were conducted with Brill for seven new cars that would have been identical to the

Nos. 77-86 were the first lightweight, high-speed, one-man cars obtained by the traction company. They were similar to Brill "Master Unit" cars in appearance. The cars were painted dark red with a black roof and a polished aluminum belt rail. The cars originally had huge front windshields, but severe glare caused them to be reduced in size several times.
Collection of John Gibb Smith, Jr.

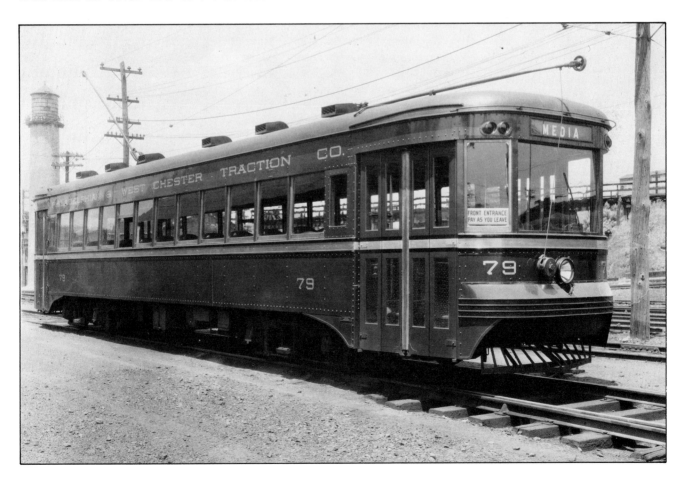

80-series cars. Brill was now desperate for orders, and the price was down to $17,000 per car. The additional cars would have been used to provide base service on the Sharon Hill and Ardmore lines. They would have permitted all non-rush hour service to be operated with one-man cars.

A formal contract with Brill was drawn up to include eight instead of seven of the proposed cars, but it was never executed because the traction company still couldn't raise the necessary funds.

Another major addition to Aronimink Transportation occurred when Montgomery Bus Company was taken over on July 1, 1936, for $100,000. This company owned 12 buses and operated four routes along Philadelphia's Main Line.

One of its routes ran from Ardmore to Gladwyne, one from 54th Street and City Avenue in Bala to Ardmore via Narberth, and two ran from 63rd Street and Lancaster Avenue in Overbrook to Garrett Hill and Strafford, serving such important mainline towns as Wynnewood, Ardmore, Haverford, Bryn Mawr, Rosemont, Villanova and Wayne.

Montgomery Bus had frequently tried to gain a connection with the Market Street Elevated, but had been blocked each time. Its lines suffered because they had no high-speed connection to Center City Philadelphia, and passengers were forced to transfer to slow streetcars at 54th Street in Bala or 63rd Street in Overbrook.

Bus operation on Lancaster Pike had begun in August 1920, when Frank J. Carlin started running two 20-passenger vehicles from Bryn Mawr to the elevated station at 63rd and Market Streets. Carlin had neglected to obtain permission from the Public Service Commission for his new route, however, and it was opposed by the traction company, PRT, the Philadelphia and Western and the Pennsylvania Railroad—a truly formidable combination.

Carlin sold out to the newly formed Montgomery Bus Company, which then received permission in 1923 to run from Rosemont to 63rd Street in Overbrook. Two years later Montgomery Bus applied for an extension to 63rd and Market Streets, which was refused. Later that year the company filed another application to run to 61st and Market Streets, but

The 80-series cars were used on the Media and West Chester lines. No. 79 was only a year old when it dropped off a passenger at Woodland Avenue station in Springfield. Collection of Fred W. Schneider, III

Nos. 83 and 84 meet on the West
Chester Division. James P. Shuman

this, too, was turned down by the Public Service Commission.

Few trips were operated on the Gladwyne route, and half-hourly service
was maintained on the Ardmore via Narberth line. The combined Garrett
Hill and Strafford lines provided 15-minute service along most of Lancaster Pike.

At the time it was purchased by Aronimink Transportation, Montgomery Bus was owned by Pennsylvania Greyhound Lines, which was controlled by the Pennsylvania Railroad.

The Garrett Hill line became Aronimink's Route Y and the Strafford
line became Route Z. The Gladwyne and Ardmore via Narberth lines
were operated separately until they were merged into Routes E and I the
following year.

These four lines increased Aronimink's income by $76,000 a year. Thirteen buses—Nos. 80-89 and 94-96—were purchased to operate the new
routes. Five more new buses came the following year. They were Nos.
100-104.

With the arrival of the 80-series cars,
all of the older cars were scrapped
except the 32 center-door cars and Nos.
40-44. The center-door cars continued
to operate most service to Ardmore
and Sharon Hill, and to supplement
rush-hour service on the West Chester
and Media lines. Collection of Fred W.
Schneider, III

By the early 1930s, there were too
many buses to load in the single lane
outside 69th Street Terminal. Traffic
congestion was also increasing, and the
traction company decided to build a
new combination bus and rail terminal.
PST

Building a New Terminal

The most important result of the activities undertaken during the
1930s to combat the Depression was the construction of a completely
new 69th Street Terminal building for the traction company and consolidation of the various companies into the Philadelphia Suburban Transportation Company.

A new terminal was desperately needed to handle the many bus routes
that had sprung up since the original trolley building was opened in 1907.
All of the buses terminating at 69th Street still had to share a single lane
next to the terminal and still had to use the sidewalk as their loading
platform. The situation was getting worse every year as more and more
buses were added to Aronimink Transportation's fleet. Up to eight buses
at a time were loading at the curbside terminus, with 41 departures
during the busiest 60-minute period.

The eight-track stubend trolley terminus had been patterned after the
traditional steam railroad terminals of the era, but it resulted in a very
inefficient operation. A maze of switches controlled from a signal tower
caused trolleys to lose time getting into and out of the terminal and
resulted in serious bottlenecks during rush hours.

Theoretically, three trolleys could load at once on each of the eight
tracks. In actual practice usually only one or two cars could load on
each track.

Even these problems, valid as they were, could scarcely be sufficient
reason to spend half a million dollars to rebuild the terminal during
Depression years when money was extremely difficult to raise. But
Merritt H. Taylor had a plan that would give him a brand new building
that would pay for itself in only 15 or 20 years.

The old terminal had virtually no space for stores or concessions. The only rentals came from a newsstand which produced a .03 percent return on the original terminal's investment. Literally all of the space was taken up by tracks and platforms and a waiting room.

The problem facing the planners was a challenging one. A new terminal had to be capable of handling at least the same number of railcars. It would have to be big enough so that 50 buses an hour could load and unload during peak periods. And it would additionally have to have enough rental space to make the building pay for its construction and operating costs.

Several plans were considered before one was finally agreed upon. The plan chosen called for a three-level building with a price tag of $800,000.

Trolleys and buses would terminate in loops in the basement. The street floor would be filled with stores producing substantial rentals, and the second floor would be occupied by new company offices and a parking lot.

Preliminary planning for this proposed building was completed in January 1934, and the next month an application was filed with the U.S. Public Works Administration requesting an $800,000 loan. The request was denied.

Unable to raise that much money by itself, the traction company was forced to choose one of the alternate plans, and by February 1936 construction was underway.

The alternate plan cost only slightly more than half as much as the original grandiose scheme, but it probably provided a better layout as far as passenger convenience was concerned. After leaving the elevated trains and climbing stairs to the main waiting room, passengers transferring to traction company trolleys or Aronimink Transportation buses would not encounter any more stairs.

While walking through the concourses between the old PRT portion of the terminal and the new trolley and bus platforms, they would pass by all of the stores that Taylor managed to find room for.

A single unloading track and two loading tracks proved to be capable of handling as many trolleys as the eight stubend tracks in the old building. The trolleys used a counterclockwise loop and the buses ran clockwise inside the trolley loop.

Only a single unloading platform and a single loading platform were designed for the buses, and it wasn't long before they became overcrowded. When this happened, several routes again began terminating on West Chester Pike alongside the terminal.

Although the new structure had been built on the same amount of land as the old one, there was even room found for two short sidings in which four cars could be stored.

The company's offices remained on the second floor of a portion of the original terminal building which was left standing. Much of the first floor of this portion was converted into a movie theater called—appropriately enough—the Terminal Theater.

The new terminal cost $486,000, which was $54,000 less than the original 1907 building had cost. It was financed through a $450,000 bank loan.

An opening day celebration was held October 26, 1936, which also marked the 150th anniversary of the founding of Upper Darby Township. Hundreds of dignitaries were invited to participate in ceremonies held in the Terminal Theater.

The Philadelphia Suburban Terminal Building Corporation was created on September 3, 1935, to raise the money to construct the new terminal

Temporary platforms were erected while the old terminal building was torn down. Collection of Ronald DeGraw

No. 80 enters one of the temporary platforms during construction. Collection of Fred W. Schneider, III

The new trolley loading platform and passenger waiting room are nearing completion. Part of the old 1907 trainshed still remains in the background. Collection of Ronald DeGraw

because the traction company was still not in good enough financial shape to swing the deal by itself. All of the stock in the new company was owned by the two Taylors, Eastern Securities, Philadelphia and Garrettford Street Railway and H. Hayes Aikens, vice president of the traction company.

The new terminal included a travel bureau, which sold Greyhound bus tickets, rail, steamship, hotel and airplane reservations and tickets for shows and sporting events. The Terminal Travel Bureau also conducted the company's lost-and-found, sold travelers' checks and travelers' insurance and arranged group bus tours during the summer. A branch of the travel bureau operated in the Ardmore trolley terminal.

Terminal Sparks a Boom

During the 29-year life of the original terminal, the entire 69th Street area had undergone an amazing transformation.

No longer did cows roam free across the road from the trolleys and the elevated trains. A tremendous building boom occurred, and it only happened because 69th Street Terminal was there.

The man responsible for developing the 69th Street shopping district

69th Street Terminal as rebuilt was a simplified track layout with a bus loop inside. A small waiting room for passengers was at the end of the trolley platform. Greyhound buses also used the terminal for a while, and one is shown here pulling out on its way to Center City. Two Liberty Bell Limited cars are loading for Allentown at the Philadelphia and Western terminal in the left background. PST

The trolley loading tracks proved too short, and soon after the new terminal was opened in 1936 the small waiting room was demolished and the platform was extended, as shown in the left foreground. Large neon signs with the Red Arrow logo appeared at both of the West Chester Pike entrances. PST

The front of the terminal as it looked in 1937, with a PRT double-decker bus heading toward Center City on Route D. PST

was realtor John H. McClatchy. McClatchy purchased 50 acres of farmland on the south side of West Chester Pike opposite the terminal in 1916 for $6,000 an acre. He boldly laid out a wide highway which ran from the main entrance of the terminal on West Chester Pike up a steep hill. This was to be 69th Street Boulevard Shopping Center. McClatchy saved the land along both sides of the boulevard for future commercial development, and all around it in the early 1920s he built homes.

To attract people to the area, he built an ornate office building on the corner of 69th Street Boulevard and West Chester Pike and decorated the outside of it with hundreds of colored lights. People came from miles around to view the brilliantly illuminated structure when it was finished in 1928. Stores and the huge Tower Theater quickly filled up 69th Street Boulevard.

At the intersection of West Chester Pike and Garrett Road, where Bond's Feed Store had once contained a traction company trolley freight station, a third theater was constructed in a large building that included apartments and a shopping arcade. More stores went up along Garrett Road and along West Chester Pike, and several more apartment buildings were constructed within walking distance of the terminal.

The real estate boom affected all of Upper Darby Township during the prosperous 1920s, chiefly because of the convenient rail and bus transportation. At the opening of the decade, Upper Darby had only 9,000 residents. Just 10 years later, its population had risen to 46,000, making

The interior of the new terminal featured pedestrian concourses and numerous shops. PST

it the largest township in the nation. Other townships along the trolley lines were growing rapidly also, particularly Haverford and Springfield, whose populations more than tripled during the 1920s.

A. Merritt Taylor had formed the Springfield Real Estate Company to acquire the original right-of-way for the Media trolley line, and the real estate company also bought up large tracts of land adjacent to the rail line, particularly in Springfield Township.

Much of this land was turned into housing developments in the 1920s and 1930s, and the houses provided new customers for the trolley line. Taylor had formed Springfield Real Estate as a personal venture, separate from the traction company.

The traction company constructed attractive stone waiting rooms at many locations along the Media, Sharon Hill and Ardmore lines to further encourage ridership.

Company Is Simplified

The other important event of 1936 was the renaming of the traction company and the consolidation of most of the various paper companies.

Anticipating such a move for more than a decade, Eastern Securities had been buying up Ardmore and Llanerch Street Railway stock and traction company stock trust certificates. By 1933 nearly all of the stock and trust certificates had been acquired. Ownership was complete by 1935, and the last of the stock certificates were retired.

On December 19, 1935, the Philadelphia and West Chester Traction Company and the Philadelphia and Garrettford Street Railway agreed to merge, with the new company called Philadelphia Suburban Transportation Company.

The Public Service Commission approved the merger on March 31, 1936, and the new company was officially incorporated April 13, automatically bringing to an end the traction company and the Philadelphia and Garrettford. The new company immediately bought all the property and franchises of the Ardmore and Llanerch Street Railway, which was then dissolved on September 1.

Aronimink Transportation could not be immediately merged into Philadelphia Suburban because there was still some preferred stock

This bus was painted silver and specially lettered in October 1936 to celebrate the opening of the new terminal and the 150th anniversary of the founding of Upper Darby Township. The company cheated somewhat on its antecedents, using 1792, which was the beginning of the Philadelphia and Lancaster Turnpike Road Company, as its date of origin. PST

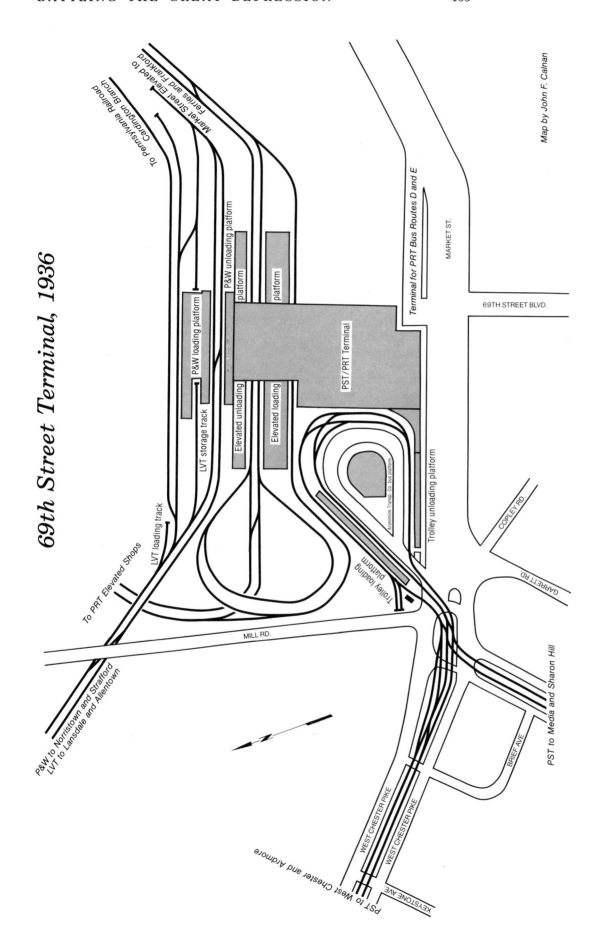

69th Street Terminal, 1936

Map by John F. Calnan

Terminal for PRT Bus Routes D and E

MARKET ST.

69TH STREET BLVD.

PST/PRT Terminal

P&W unloading platform

platform

platform

P&W loading platform

Elevated unloading

Elevated loading

LVT storage track

LVT loading track

To PRT Elevated Shops

To Pennsylvania Railroad Cardington Branch

Market Street Elevated to Ferries and Frankford

Aronimink Transp. Co. bus platform

Trolley unloading platform

Trolley loading platform

COPLEY RD.

GARRETT RD.

MILL RD.

P&W to Norristown and Strafford
LVT to Lansdale and Allentown

BRIEF AVE.

PST to Media and Sharon Hill

WEST CHESTER PIKE

WEST CHESTER PIKE

KEYSTONE AVE.

PST to West Chester and Ardmore

outstanding which it had issued to purchase the other bus companies in 1930. When the last of that stock was redeemed, Aronimink Transportation was brought into the merger on December 31, 1941.

Philadelphia Suburban reached a strong enough financial position by 1938 so that it could acquire the new terminal and dissolve the Terminal Building Corporation, which it did on December 29, 1938.

This left only Eastern Securities Company, and it no longer had any reason for existing, although it now held all of the stock of Philadelphia Suburban. Eastern Securities was therefore dissolved February 26, 1943, after it turned over to its shareholders the Philadelphia Suburban stock.

The new name of the merged company more clearly reflected the direction in which the company's expansion moves were taking it. With its four different trolley lines, the name of Philadelphia and West Chester Traction was no longer very descriptive of the company's activities. The same logic applied to Aronimink Transportation. The initial bus line to Aronimink was now only one of 15 bus routes being operated by the company. And it also made no sense to continue operating the bus routes under a subsidiary company.

The red trolleys and buses had expanded to cover most of the main line and Eastern Delaware County, and the new name—Philadelphia Suburban Transportation Company—more clearly reflected this expansion.

The new name was a mouthful, however, and the Taylors felt the need for a short, punchy, easy-to-remember nickname. The Philadelphia advertising firm of Al Paul Lefton Co., Inc., in March 1937 designed a new

Bus No. 103 (center) arrived in 1937. In the foreground, a PRT Route E bus is bound for Germantown via Woodside Park. A double-decker on Route D awaits departure to Center City. The PRT parking lot is in the background. PST

emblem using a red and cream arrow enclosed in a circle and bearing the words "Red Arrow Lines." The attractive emblem was quickly placed on the sides of all buses and trolleys and on all timetables and public notices. Within a very short time everybody was calling the system "Red Arrow."

A Tribute to Taylor

A. Merritt Taylor's health had continued to decline during the Depression years, and he died on June 6, 1937, at the age of 63. At precisely 4:30 p.m. on June 8, all Red Arrow buses and trolleys came to a stop for one minute as a mark of respect for the company's former president.

Union representation came to Red Arrow for the first time when contracts were signed on July 8, 1937. The motormen and conductors were represented by Sam Harvey Lodge No. 998 of the Brotherhood of Railroad Trainmen and the maintenance employees formed Red Arrow Local No. 1, Unit 15, of the Brotherhood of Railroad Shop Crafts of America.

Red Arrow employees had fared better than many other American workers during the Depression. In 1930, the hourly pay for operating

The new "Red Arrow Lines" logo quickly appeared on all buses and trolleys. The company also undertook a series of advertising posters using the new logo, such as the one on the front of this center-door car. PST

employees had been 60 cents with no vacation and a 58.5-hour work week. By 1939 the hourly wage was 70 cents with one-week vacation and 50.5 hours of work a week.

When trolleys first started operating in 1895, motormen and conductors were paid 12½ cents an hour. Taylor increased this to 14 cents as soon as he took over in 1899 and another two cents the following year. By 1916, wages had climbed to 29 cents an hour, and had shot up to 51 cents by the end of World War I three years later.

The company's financial position permitted wages to be raised 8.3 percent on August 1, 1936, and another 8.7 percent on September 1, 1937, to partly make up for the wage reductions which had occurred in 1931 and 1932.

During the late 1930s, Red Arrow continued to expand its bus system. Route O was extended from Swarthmore to Chester under a joint arrangement with Southern Pennsylvania Bus Company on February 27, 1938. The expanded Route O was an immediate success, producing annual revenue of $17,000. Buses operated every 30 minutes during the midday and every 12 minutes in peak periods.

Route I was extended from Ardmore to Bryn Mawr in 1939.

A new route was established September 5, 1939, from 54th Street and City Avenue in Bala to West Manayunk and Ardmore, operating only six round trips a day. This became Route K. The rights were acquired from Philadelphia Rapid Transit Company. In return, Red Arrow gave PRT Route G, the Morton bus line. Service on Route G by Red Arrow ceased on September 4. Route G was the only Red Arrow bus route by the late 1930s which was not producing a profit.

The 80-series quickly proved to be superb cars, and Red Arrow ran them as often as possible. No. 78 slows for Beatty Road crossing on the Media Division. James P. Shuman

Within a few years, the arrow in the logo grew a long tail, as seen on this two-car train of center-door cars. David H. Cope

No. 80 speeds over the bridge at the Ridley Creek Substation on the West Chester line. The building was formerly a powerhouse. The bridge abutments were built for double-track, although none of the West Chester line was ever double-tracked west of Westgate Hills. David H. Cope

Twelve new buses—Nos. 105-116—were acquired in 1939. At the end of 1939, Red Arrow had 82 buses and 46 active rail cars on its roster. All of the old Brill and Jewett interurbans had been retired, and one of the center-door cars had been destroyed in a collision.

Red Arrow had managed to weather the Great Depression surprisingly well, certainly much better than most of the nation's transportation companies.

By the end of 1939 it boasted six percent more zone passengers than it had carried in 1930. No figures were kept on precisely how many actual riders Red Arrow carried. Instead, each individual zone fare was counted as one "zone passenger." Thus a passenger riding the single zone from 69th Street to Ardmore was counted once, but someone riding the five zones to West Chester was counted five times. This system is no longer used.

PRT, by comparison, was carrying 25 percent fewer zone passengers

No. 80 picks up a passenger at Edgemont, inbound from West Chester. The trolley line ran very close to West Chester Pike. David H. Cope

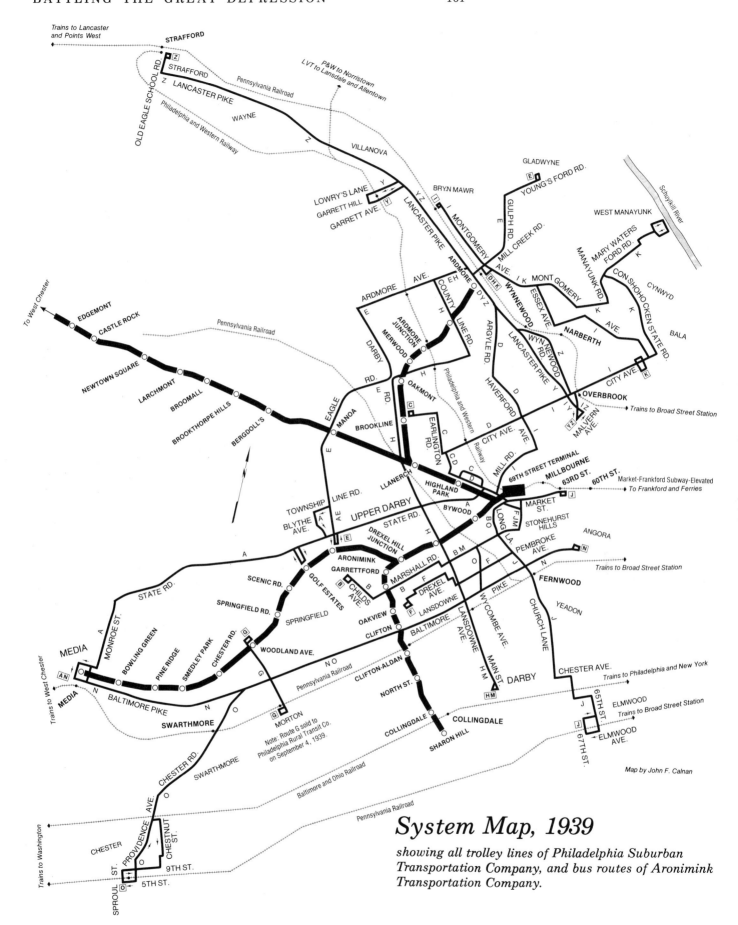

System Map, 1939

showing all trolley lines of Philadelphia Suburban Transportation Company, and bus routes of Aronimink Transportation Company.

than it had carried 10 years earlier. Total revenue by the end of the decade for Red Arrow was only 7.5 percent under the 1931 high, despite the continuation of the lower fares.

Daily vehicle mileage for the entire system increased about 33 percent over 1930, while operating expenses and fixed charges per vehicle showed a decrease of 26 percent over the same period.

During the 10-year period, 70 new buses and 10 new trolleys had been purchased at a total cost of $801,000. All of the improvements and economy measures during the Depression had resulted in annual savings of $378,000 in operating costs, and that meant the difference between profit and loss for several years.

The traction company had been forced to suspend dividends on its common stock for the first time in 1933, but interest payments and preferred stock dividends were paid during every year of the Depression.

Late in 1899, when A. Merritt Taylor had been in control of the traction company for less than a year, he remarked to a friend: "I don't mind saying, I believe I have had the honor of saving the company from bankruptcy."

Not only had he saved it, he had also turned it into one of the finest and most prosperous suburban transit systems in the nation, capable of withstanding the worst economic disaster in history.

Of all the Brill and Jewett interurban cars (except Nos. 40-44), only No. 34 survived the 1930s. It was converted to a snowplow and work car and finally scrapped in 1948. James P. Shuman

Chapter 9

World War and Boom Times, 1940–1948

RED ARROW'S RAPID EXPANSION of its bus system during the 1930s had been so successful that in 1940, for the first time, the income from the bus lines was slightly higher than the total trolley income. Route E was extended southward to Darby in the same year, and five more buses—Nos. 117-121—were acquired.

Flushed with the success of its new 69th Street Terminal, which opened in 1936, the company began planning the following year for a new bus and trolley terminal in Ardmore. The centerpiece of the complex would have been a movie theater, and negotiations were conducted with the Stanley Company of America to lease and operate the theater. In 1938 the Stanley Company withdrew from negotiations.

Once more, in 1943, a new $350,000 Ardmore Terminal was proposed, to include a restaurant, a theater, shops, a waiting room, bus and trolley platforms and offices. But it was never built.

The huge old Ardmore trainshed, in the meanwhile, was torn down in 1938 because it was in poor condition. The waiting room remained, and a simple canopy was built over the platform to protect passengers.

In 1939, land was purchased adjacent to the Ardmore trolley terminus for a new bus garage to accommodate all of the routes operating to Ardmore and other parts of the main line. The garage, fronting on Crickett Terrace, cost $45,500 and opened in 1940. This permitted the closing of the small garage in Bryn Mawr which Aronimink Transportation had inherited from Montgomery Bus in 1936. The Ardmore garage was necessary because the Bryn Mawr facility was inadequate and because the main garage at Llanerch wasn't big enough to handle the expanded bus system.

On June 4, 1940, Red Arrow ordered eight lightweight, one-man, high-speed trolleys from Brill, costing $24,200 each, with Brill providing the financing. On December 3, the order was increased to 10 cars. They were to be used to provide all off-peak service on the Ardmore and Sharon Hill lines. These streamlined "Brilliners," delivered in September 1941, were the last trolley cars ever built by the J.G. Brill Company, which had been the world's largest builder of electric railway cars.

When the new cars were ordered, a decision was made to start the numbering system over again for all new trolleys and buses, and these 10 cars became Nos. 1-10. Five buses ordered early in 1941 were mysteriously numbered 150-154, but 15 more buses later in the year became Nos. 1-10 and Nos. 21-25. The buses cost approximately $12,000 each.

The arrival of the Brilliners meant that off-peak service on all four trolley lines could now be operated by the faster, more economical one-man cars instead of the slower center-door cars that required both a

Five new buses built by American Car and Foundry arrived in 1940. PST

motorman and a conductor. When the new cars arrived, Red Arrow immediately scrapped nine of the original ten 1919 center-door cars, Nos. 45-46 and Nos. 48-54. No. 47 was renumbered to become No. 55. The original No. 55 had been destroyed in a wreck in 1935. Within months, Red Arrow was to regret the loss of these nine cars.

Scrapping the nine center-door cars less than two months before the bombing of Pearl Harbor was clear evidence that Red Arrow, like most transit companies, wasn't ready when World War II burst upon it. Ridership suddenly jumped by 50 percent from 1941 to 1942, and there were not nearly enough men and vehicles to keep pace with the rapidly spiraling growth.

Between 1941 and 1943 patronage doubled, and by 1945 it had gone up another two million, reaching 41.7 million zone passengers a year.

To handle the extra traffic, new substations were built at 69th Street in 1943 and at Milltown in 1944. Two years after the war, another substation was opened at Florida Park just west of Newtown Square and the old Ridley Creek facility was abandoned.

The beginning of the war found Red Arrow with 47 trolleys and 94 buses. New trolley cars and buses were impossible to obtain during the war, so in desperation Red Arrow in October 1942 bought three Hog Island-type trolleys from the Philadelphia Transportation Company, successor to the PRT, that had been built in 1918 and 1919. Red Arrow paid $1,500 each for the cars, and spent another $5,000 each to rehabilitate them. They became Nos. 20-22, later changed to Nos. 25-27.

The cars were officially rated for 46 seated passengers and 50 standees, but their side-bench seating arrangement provided a great deal of standing room and they often carried more than 150 passengers.

New and used buses were virtually unobtainable. The U.S. Office of Defense Transportation assigned new vehicles to properties on the basis of need, and Red Arrow's fleet was in such good shape that it was able to obtain only 10 more buses during the war. Nos. 11-20 arrived in 1944. They were the first General Motors buses the company had ever owned, and for the next quarter of a century Red Arrow bought nothing but GM buses.

The war brought serious gasoline and tire shortages. Pleasure driving was banned in the east in 1943, and people swarmed aboard Red Arrow's buses and railcars. The recently expanded Route O to Chester proved extremely profitable as thousands of workers were carried daily to the big Sun Ship and Dry Dock Corporation in Chester.

Red Arrow leased a parking lot just outside 69th Street Terminal to store buses during off-peak hours. This conserved a great deal of fuel by eliminating deadheading to the Llanerch garage after each rush hour.

Skip-stops were instituted by the Office of Defense Transportation, and three cuts in bus service were ordered because of the fuel shortage. The third cut, effective May 24, 1943, forced Red Arrow to curtail bus service by 30 percent, despite the fact that patronage had increased 100 percent in the past two years. The only way Red Arrow could comply with this last order was to eliminate some routes altogether and run buses only during rush hours on some others. Service was completely eliminated on Routes B, C, N, Y and Z. By the fall of 1945, however, all of

One of the newest buses posed with one of the 1932 trolleys in 1940. The bus sports an experimental paint scheme and a tail has been added for the first time to the arrow logo. The railcar still bears the original logo, an arrow in a circle. PST

the cuts had been rescinded and full service had been almost completely restored on all the routes.

Even more serious than these problems, however, was the lack of manpower. With draft calls going higher each month, Red Arrow found itself without enough men to run its buses and trolleys.

The Distaff Staff

In February 1943, it started hiring women to collect fares on the trolleys and called them "conductorettes." Soon the shortage of men was so severe that women also began operating the trolleys, and by the end of the war more than 75 women were employed.

Although the women generally performed as well as their male counterparts, two of them were involved in a bizarre accident on December 6, 1944. A center-door car, with a female motorman and a "conductorette," was making a short-turn trip to Oakmont at the end of the evening rush hour to relieve the overcrowded Ardmore cars. The car had reached Oakmont and unloaded all of its passengers. Both women were outside the trolley, preparing to return to the Llanerch carbarn. One was changing the pole and the other had just thrown the switch to cross over.

As the trolley pole hit the wire, however, the car gave a sudden lurch, rumbled onto the crossover and ran away toward Llanerch without its crew. It would have been an amusing incident except that the big car, gaining speed as it rolled down a hill, crashed into the rear of a lightweight car that was loading at Park Road just west of Llanerch. Fourteen persons were injured and the two trolleys were temporarily out of service at a time when every piece of equipment was desperately needed.

No. 75 paused in the old Ardmore trainshed a few weeks before it was torn down in 1938. The second track had been removed many years before. John J. Bowman, Jr.

The original Ardmore station building
remained for another two decades,
minus much of its initial elegance.
E. Everett Edwards

Female employees were "retired" as the men began to return from the
war, and the last of the women departed on January 14, 1946. The women
were paid about 25 percent less than the men.

By the end of the war there had been changes in several bus lines and
one more route had been created. The new line was Route X, which ran to
Media via Pilgrim Gardens. Route A was then cut back to Aronimink,
and no longer ran to Media.

Route J to Yeadon and southwest Philadelphia now began its run outside 69th Street Terminal rather than at 63rd and Market Streets as it
had since it was created in 1930. Route K was discontinued between West
Manayunk and Ardmore and was instead extended across the Schuylkill
River to Manayunk. Route Z was extended a quarter of a mile to terminate at the Strafford station of the Philadelphia and Western.

The war had also marked the first time that regular 15-minute service
was run on the West Chester rail division. Previously, half-hour service
had been considered sufficient because the West Chester Pike area hadn't
developed nearly as rapidly as the territory served by the other bus and
rail lines.

But beginning in 1942, trolleys ran to Larchmont (1.2 miles east of
Newtown Square) every 15 minutes and to West Chester every 30

The first of the 1941 Brilliners is
delivered on a Pennsylvania Railroad
flatcar, then transferred via temporary
track to the trolley line behind the
Llanerch carbarn. David H. Cope

minutes from 5:30 a.m. until midnight. Many two-car trains were operated. In addition, short-turn cars were run to Westgate Hills to handle rush-hour crowds.

Ridership was so heavy that 15-minute service was also maintained to Larchmont on Saturdays, although every 30 minutes was still considered adequate for Sundays in 1942. By the end of the war, however, 15-minute service was being run all the way to West Chester on Saturdays and as far as Larchmont on Sundays.

The J.G. Brill Company refused to build PCC cars, depending instead upon its own Brilliner design. The 10 Red Arrow Brilliners were the last railcars ever built by Brill. The cars arrived with the revised logo. PST

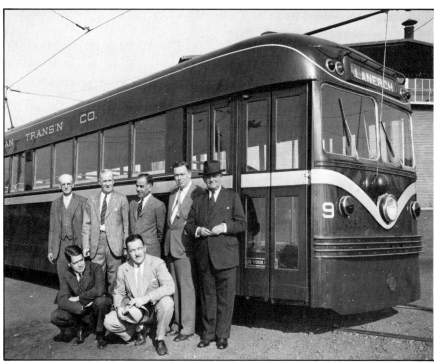

Posing with brand-new Brilliner No. 9 in 1941 were Red Arrow Corporate Secretary Charles S. Taylor, 3rd, and Robert Dagleish of Westinghouse (kneeling); and (left to right) Otto Kinsler, Red Arrow's master mechanic; Ridge Moon of Westinghouse; Vice President John R. McCain; President Merritt H. Taylor; and Vice President H. Hayes Aikens. PST

A stub-end siding was installed at Larchmont for short-turn cars in 1946, and the only passing siding between Larchmont and Westgate Hills—at Brookthorpe Hills—was considerably lengthened.

Taylor served as a consultant to the War Department's Transportation Corps during the war, and in 1944 he was named chief of transportation for the Allied Commission in Italy. Red Arrow was managed by First Vice President John R. McCain during Taylor's absence. McCain had been promoted after H. Hayes Aikens died on February 7, 1942. Aikens

The Brilliners were elegant in their original paint scheme. The body was dark red with a wide silver stripe flanked by narrow black stripes; the roof was black edged with a silver stripe. William C. Janssen

Red Arrow's excellent transportation routes were largely responsible for the influx of new residents into Eastern Delaware County following World War II. This photo was taken by the "Upper Darby News" to accompany a story pointing out the advantages of living in the western suburbs. Cyril J. Nugent

had been with the company since 1898. He became corporate secretary in 1905 and was appointed vice president in 1909.

Like his father, Merritt H. Taylor was also active in other companies besides Red Arrow. He was president of Pennsylvania and Southern Gas Company and the Allied Gas Company of Illinois. He was a director of Texas Public Service Company, Peoples Power and Light Company and Great Lakes Utility Company.

A Time for Expansion

Even the war years did not stop Red Arrow from continuing attempts to expand its system. Discussions were held with PTC in April 1942 concerning the possibility of purchasing that company's Darby, Media and Chester bus routes. In July 1945, Red Arrow was approached by National Power and Light Company concerning the possible purchase of the Lehigh Valley Transit Company. LVT operated a high-speed interurban line from 69th Street Terminal to Allentown, using trackage rights over the Philadelphia and Western from 69th Street to Norristown, and an extensive network of local rail and bus routes in Allentown, Bethlehem and Easton.

"After analyzing the earnings statements of LVT for the past five years, it was the consensus of opinion that we should make no offer at this time," according to Red Arrow's board of directors' minute books.

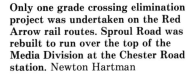

Only one grade crossing elimination project was undertaken on the Red Arrow rail routes. Sproul Road was rebuilt to run over the top of the Media Division at the Chester Road station. Newton Hartman

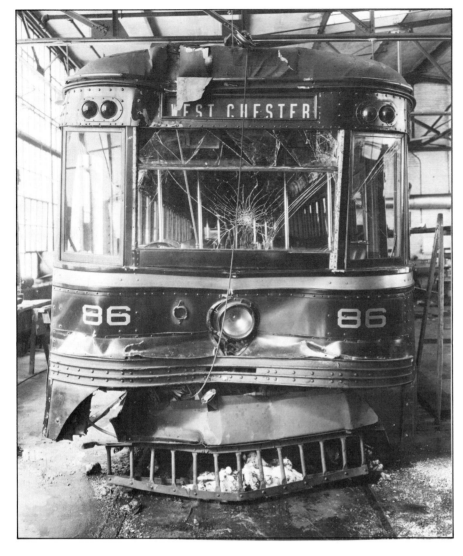

No. 86 crashed into an automobile on the West Chester Division in 1941. Red Arrow's safety record was generally very good, despite the dangers of a lengthy and fast single-track line. PST

Carbarn employees lined up examples of all four types of equipment serving the trolley lines in 1941. Five of the 40-series Jewett cars, 22 of the center-door cars and 10 each of the 80-series and Brilliners comprised the roster as Red Arrow entered World War II. David H. Cope

Short-turn trips were operated to many points on the rail system to accommodate the great number of wartime riders. Jewett No. 41 is heading to Oakmont. Right behind it is Hog Island No. 20 en route to Drexel-brook. A two-car train of center-door cars is arriving from Oakmont. The Schmidt's beer clock shows the time as 5:21 p.m. on a summer wartime rush hour. David H. Cope

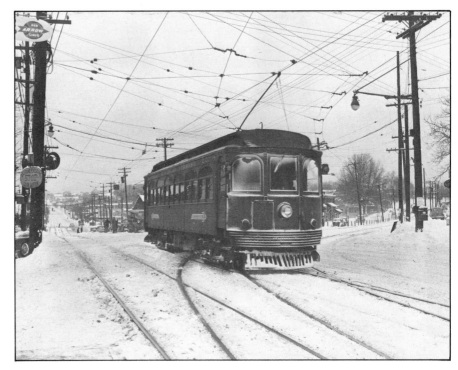

The five Jewett 40-series cars, built in 1914, saw very active service during and immediately after World War II, despite their age. No. 44 passes Llanerch Junction on its way to West Chester. David H. Cope

The 40 series were handsome cars, and were kept in good condition by Red Arrow. No. 42 sleeps away the midday on a siding just outside 69th Street Terminal, waiting for the evening rush hour. David H. Cope

No. 42 approaches Llanerch Junction on an inbound trip from West Chester. David H. Cope

No. 76 departs from 69th Street Terminal on a short-turn to Clifton on the Sharon Hill Division. Lester K. Wismer

No. 56 at Drexel Hill Junction en route to Sharon Hill. James P. Shuman

No. 77 inbound from Media approaching Drexel Hill Junction. James P. Shuman

Red Arrow could supplement its rail fleet during World War II with only three used Hog Island cars acquired from Philadelphia Transportation Company. Slow and uncomfortable, they were used only for short-turn service. This car is destined for Westgate Hills.
David H. Cope

The spartan interiors of the Hog Island cars included long side benches and handholds for standees. They were good crowd-swallowers, sometimes carrying as many as 150 passengers.
PST

Taylor had been moving since 1943, however, to acquire the Philadelphia and Western, which operated rail lines to Norristown and Strafford as well as a small bus subsidiary. P&W had been forced into bankruptcy by the Depression in 1934. As early as 1939, bond salesmen began trying to convince Taylor to gain control of P&W by purchasing its bonds. Taylor hesitated, but in 1943 he received an offer he apparently could not resist. He purchased $800,000 of P&W's bonds at 40 cents on the dollar. This amounted to about one-third of the railroad's bonds, and it immediately made Taylor a key figure in the company's reorganization. He also began purchasing P&W stock.

P&W's officers wanted to keep Taylor out. They took their fight to court, but lost. Red Arrow finally held enough stock to give it control of the P&W, and on October 1, 1946, Taylor was elected as president of P&W. All of the Red Arrow officers and directors were elected to the same positions with P&W, and the old P&W management was dismissed.

Tickets which were good on either P&W or Red Arrow were issued beginning in 1947. The companies could not be merged, however, until Red Arrow acquired all of the P&W stock. In April 1948, Red Arrow borrowed $300,000 to purchase more P&W stock, and by mid-1948 owned about two-thirds of the stock.

Merritt H. Taylor bade farewell to the last of the conductorettes—Mrs. Ruth Black and Mrs. Estelle Scanlin—on January 14, 1946. Head of the conductorettes was Mrs. Elizabeth Harding (left), who remained with Red Arrow for another quarter of a century. PST

All bus maintenance was performed at
the Llanerch garage, which was
tremendously overtaxed during the
war years. PST

Financially, the war years had been very good to Red Arrow, resulting
in a net profit of $222,000 for 1944. This dropped slightly in 1945, then
climbed to $468,000 in 1946. Profits for 1947 were $403,000 and for 1948
$296,000.

The prosperous war years had permitted many of the company's outstanding bonds to be paid off ahead of time and put Red Arrow in a
stronger financial position than ever before in its history. The cost of the
Brilliners was paid off by 1945, as well as everything owed on the bus
purchases.

The company bought new buses as soon as it could after the war. Nos.
26-35 arrived in 1946. As production of transit vehicles got back to
normal after the war, 21 more buses—Nos. 36-56—came in 1947 and
another 20—Nos. 57-76—in 1948.

Extensive renovations were made to 69th Street Terminal in 1946,
providing additional space for stores which produced an extra $25,000 a
year in rentals. The $160,000 renovation included the removal of a large
restaurant which had originally been built under the trolley loop and a
rearrangement of the pedestrian corridors. Gross income from terminal
rentals had risen from $58,000 in 1937 to $135,000 in 1947, which meant
the terminal was producing a 10.9 percent return on its investment.

All-night hourly trolley service to Media was inaugurated in March
1947. Previously, service was operated only as far as Springfield between
2:00 a.m. and 5:00 a.m.

Even with the war over, ridership continued to climb slightly. Zone
passengers went from 41.7 million in 1945 to 42.1 million in 1946 and 42
million in 1947. Ridership hit an all-time high of 42.5 million in 1948.

Red Arrow opened its centennial year of 1948 with the announcement
that it would spend $1 million on improvements during the year, includ-

ing the purchase of 14 new trolley cars. The postwar exodus to suburbia was engulfing most of Red Arrow's territory, and ridership during 1948 was higher than ever in the company's history.

"The building of homes during the past two years in the territory served by this company has been phenomenal, and today there are many more thousands of houses under construction," said Taylor.

Red Arrow appeared to be a company with a truly unlimited future. At a time when other transit companies throughout the country were planning to abandon their rail lines, Red Arrow was announcing that it was firmly committed to rail and, moreover, was buying new cars. Expansion of the company was continuing with the takeover of the Philadelphia and Western.

The little country trolley line to West Chester that A. Merritt Taylor had gained control of in 1899 had been transformed into one of the most successful suburban transportation companies in the United States.

As originally built, the 1936 bus terminal had an additional lane next to the loading platform so that buses could pull around one another if necessary. Only four buses at a time could load at the platform, however, and the increase in passengers caused severe overcrowding. In 1948, the additional lane was eliminated and the loading platform was lengthened so that five buses could load simultaneously. PST

Despite a doubling of ridership, Red Arrow was only able to obtain 10 new buses during the war. Nos. 11-20 arrived in 1944, seating 40 passengers each. PST

The bus loading platform on West Chester Pike just outside the terminal in 1947. PST

Nos. 20 and 22, together with three others, were built in 1941. They are posed in front of the Llanerch bus garage. The West Chester Division tracks are on the right. PST

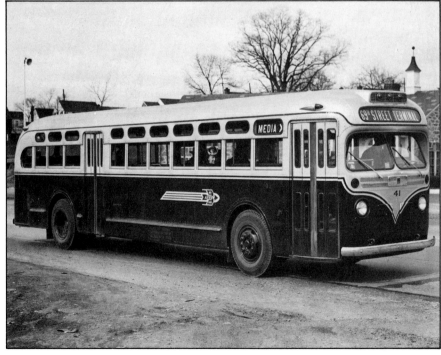

No. 41 was a 1947 General Motors bus. Twenty-one new buses arrived in 1947 and another 20 in 1948. PST

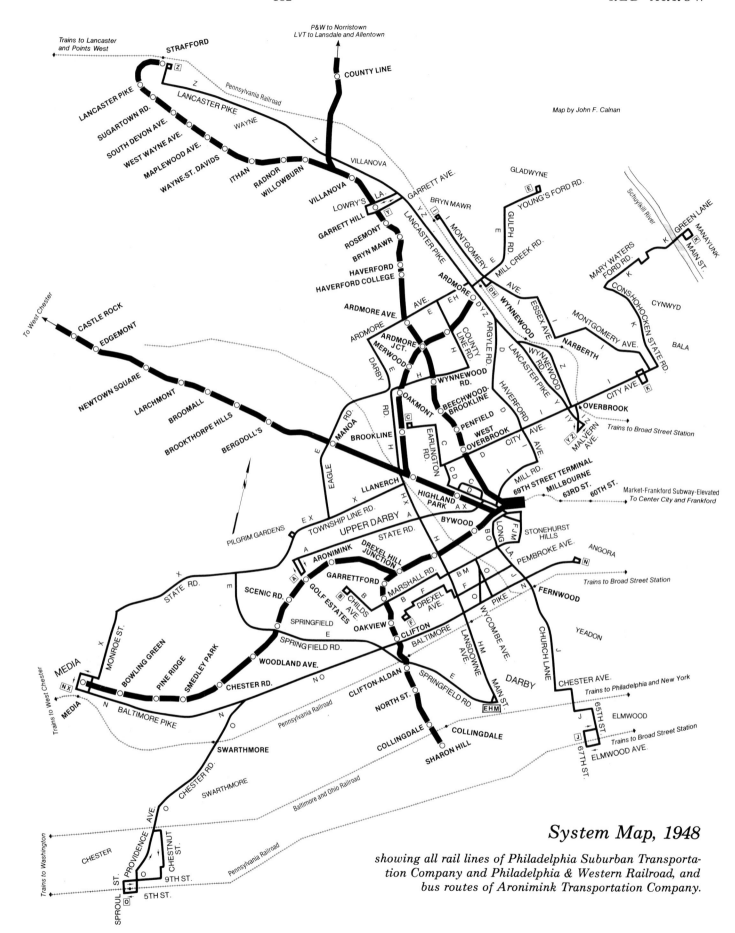

Trains to Lancaster and Points West

STRAFFORD

P&W to Norristown
LVT to Lansdale and Allentown

COUNTY LINE

Map by John F. Calnan

LANCASTER PIKE
SUGARTOWN RD.
SOUTH DEVON AVE.
WEST WAYNE AVE.
MAPLEWOOD AVE.
WAYNE-ST. DAVIDS
ITHAN
RADNOR
WILLOWBURN
VILLANOVA
LOWRY'S
GARRETT HILL
ROSEMONT
BRYN MAWR
HAVERFORD
HAVERFORD COLLEGE

Pennsylvania Railroad
LANCASTER PIKE
WAYNE
Z
VILLANOVA
GARRETT AVE.
BRYN MAWR
GLADWYNE
YOUNG'S FORD RD.

Schuylkill River
GREEN LANE
MANAYUNK
MAIN ST.
MARY WATERS FORD RD.
CONSHOHOCKEN STATE RD.
CYNWYD

To West Chester

CASTLE ROCK
EDGEMONT
NEWTOWN SQUARE
LARCHMONT
BROOMALL
BROOKTHORPE HILLS
BERGDOLL'S

ARDMORE AVE.
ARDMORE
DARBY
ARDMORE JCT.
MERWOOD
WYNNEWOOD RD.
OAKMONT
BROOKLINE
MANOA
LLANERCH

COUNTY LINE RD.
ARGYLE RD.
WYNNEWOOD
BEECHWOOD-BROOKLINE
PENFIELD
WEST OVERBROOK
EARLINGTON RD.
HIGHLAND PARK

GULPH RD.
MILL CREEK RD.
WYNNEWOOD
NARBERTH
MONTGOMERY AVE.
BALA
ESSEX AVE.
LANCASTER PIKE
HAVERFORD
CITY AVE.
OVERBROOK
CITY AVE.

Trains to Broad Street Station

MALVERN AVE.
MILL RD.
69TH STREET TERMINAL
MILLBOURNE
63RD ST.
60TH ST.
Market-Frankford Subway-Elevated
To Center City and Frankford

PILGRIM GARDENS
TOWNSHIP LINE RD.
UPPER DARBY
STATE RD.
BYWOOD
STONEHURST HILLS
LONG LA.
PEMBROKE AVE.
ANGORA
Trains to Broad Street Station

ARONIMINK
DREXEL HILL JUNCTION
GARRETTFORD
GOLF ESTATES
CHILDS AVE.
OAKVIEW
MARSHALL RD.
DREXEL AVE.
CLIFTON
BALTIMORE
FERNWOOD
YEADON
WYCOMBE AVE.
LANSDOWNE AVE.
MAIN ST.
CHURCH LANE
DARBY

SCENIC RD.
STATE RD.
MONROE ST.
SPRINGFIELD
SPRINGFIELD RD.
WOODLAND AVE.

MEDIA
BOWLING GREEN
PINE RIDGE
SMEDLEY PARK
CHESTER RD.

MEDIA
BALTIMORE PIKE
Trains to West Chester

SWARTHMORE
Pennsylvania Railroad
CHESTER RD.
SWARTHMORE
Baltimore and Ohio Railroad

CLIFTON-ALDAN
NORTH ST.
SPRINGFIELD RD.
COLLINGDALE
SHARON HILL
COLLINGDALE

CHESTER AVE.
Trains to Philadelphia and New York
65TH ST.
ELMWOOD
67TH ST.
ELMWOOD AVE.
Trains to Broad Street Station

CHESTER
PROVIDENCE AVE.
CHESTNUT ST.
9TH ST.
SPROUL ST.
5TH ST.
Trains to Washington
Pennsylvania Railroad

System Map, 1948

showing all rail lines of Philadelphia Suburban Transportation Company and Philadelphia & Western Railroad, and bus routes of Aronimink Transportation Company.

No. 20 inbound at Brookline station on the Ardmore Division in 1948. The three Hog Island cars, purchased as a wartime measure, operated for another 10 years. David H. Cope

A steam locomotive is shifting freight cars on the Pennsylvania Railroad's Newtown Square branch at Llanerch in 1948, as No. 41 operates to Westgate Hills. David H. Cope

Philadelphia Suburban Transportation Co.
And Its Predecessors

Car No.	Fleet Size	Type	Year Acquired	Builder	Length	Width	Height	Seats
1, 2, 4, 6, 7, 9, 10, and two others	9	Steam dummy	7/95	Unknown				
100-114	15	Single-truck open	1895	Lamokin	30' 0"	8' 4"	11' 7"	50
1-3	3	Single-truck closed	1896	P&WCT	About 25'	8' 0"	11' 6"	28
4	1	Single-truck open, rebuilt to closed	1896	Lamokin				
5-6	2	Single-truck closed	1896	Brill	31' 0"	7' 6"	11' 5"	32
7-12	6	Double-truck closed	1898	Jackson & Sharp	39' 0"	8' 2"	12' 0"	40
13	1	Double-truck closed	1899	Jackson & Sharp	39' 0"	8' 2"	12' 0"	40
101-105	5	Double-truck open	1900	American	40' 1"			70
14-16	3	Double-truck closed	1902	Brill	41' 0"	8' 4"		40
106-107	2	Double-truck open	1903	Brill	41' 7"	8' 5"	12' 8"	70
17-23	7	Interurban	6/06	Brill	45' 3"	8' 6"	12' 3"	48
24-30	7	Interurban	1907	Jewett	48' 6"	8' 8"	12' 3"	52
31-32	2	Interurban	1907	Jewett	51' 3"	8' 8"	12' 3"	56
33-37	5	Interurban	1912	Jewett	44' 6"	8' 10"	12' 3"	48
38-39	2	Interurban	1913	Jewett	51' 3"	8' 8"	12' 3"	56
40-44	5	Interurban	1914	Jewett	44' 6"	8' 10"	12' 3"	48
45-54	10	Center-door car	1919	Brill	47' 3"	8' 10"	12' 5"	57
55-64	10	Center-door car	1925	Brill	47' 10"	8' 7"	12' 5"	62
65-76	12	Center-door car	1926	Brill	47' 10"	8' 7"	12' 5"	62
77-81	5	80-series	3/32	Brill	49' 2"	8' 10"	10' 6"	61
82-86	5	80-series	6/32	Brill	49' 2"	8' 10"	10' 6"	61
1-10	10	Brilliner	9/41	Brill	48' 4"	8' 10"	10' 0"	58
20-22	3	Hog Island car	1942	Brill	45' 6"	8' 6"	12' 4"	46

Roster of Passenger Cars to 1948

Cost Per Car	Weight	Trucks	Motors	Wheels	Disposition	Notes
$300					Scrapped between 1896 and 1899.	Originally built in 1863 for Frankford and Southwark Passenger Railroad Co. 10-bench open cars.
	23,000	McGuire	2-WH68	30″	Four cars sold 1900 to Inland Traction Co., Souderton, Pa.; five sold 1901 to Cumberland Valley Traction Co.; four sold 1901 to Conestoga Traction Co. Nos. 111 and 114 scrapped 1905.	
		Hardy and Lary (later Brill 21-E)	2-WH68	30″	Scrapped by 1900.	Rebuilt from old horsecar bodies acquired in 1895.
		McGuire (later Brill 21-E)	2-WH68	30″	Retired 1900; rebuilt in 1902 as work car No. 02. Sold 1926.	Acquired secondhand; origin unknown. Open car, rebuilt to closed car 1898.
	22,000	Brill 21-E	2-WH68	30″	Retired 1907. No. 5 scrapped; No. 6 converted to emergency car; scrapped about 1933.	
$4,700	34,000	Peckham 14-B (later Brill 27-G)	4-WH68	33″	No. 9 sold 1907 to Nevada Interurban; No. 11 sold 1907 to a Johnstown, Pa., company. Rest retired 1910. Nos. 7, 10, 12 scrapped 1912. No. 8 retained as work car, scrapped 1933.	Acquired for West Chester extension; contained smoking compartments.
$4,700	34,000	Peckham 14-B (later Brill 27-G)	4-WH68	33″	Sold 1907 to Nevada Interurban.	Almost identical to Nos. 7-12.
	31,000	Brill 27-G	4-WH68	33″	Sold 1912.	14-bench open cars.
$12,300	34,000	Brill 24-E	4-WH68	33″	No. 14 converted to emergency car in 1914, scrapped 1926. No. 15 scrapped 1914. No. 16 converted to line car, scrapped 1922.	Acquired for Ardmore line; contained smoking compartments.
$10,300	27,000	Brill 27-G	4-WH68	33″	Scrapped 1924.	14-bench open cars.
	68,000	Baldwin MCB	4-GE73	34″	No. 18 retired 1925. No. 17 converted to emergency car in 1926. All cars scrapped by 1933.	
	55,000	Baldwin MCB	4-GE73	34″	Nos. 24-26 and 29-30 scrapped 1931. Nos. 27-28 scrapped 1936.	
	60,000	Baldwin Curved Equalizer	4-GE73	34″	Retired 1933.	
	50,000	Baldwin Curved Equalizer		34″	Nos. 36-37 retired 1927. Nos. 33 and 35 scrapped 1936. No. 34 converted to snowplow; scrapped 1941; body used as shed at Llanerch.	
$12,000	60,000	Baldwin Curved Equalizer	4-GE205	34″	Scrapped 1933.	Acquired for Media line.
	50,000	Baldwin Curved Equalizer	4-GE203L (later Brill 77-E)	33″	All in active service in 1948.	Equipped with high-speed trucks in 1927.
$17,500	58,000	Brill 27MCB-3X	4-GE203L	33″	Nos. 45-46, 48-54 scrapped 1941. No. 47 renumbered to No. 55 in 1941.	First all-steel cars.
$18,600	59,000	Brill 27MCB-3X	4-GE203L	33″	No. 55 destroyed in wreck in 1935. Nos. 56-64 in active service in 1948.	
	59,000	Brill 27MCB-3X	4-GE203L	33″	All in active service in 1948.	
$19,500	42,000	Brill 89E-1	4-GE301B	26″	All in active service in 1948.	First high-speed, one-man lightweight cars.
$18,100	42,000	Brill 89E-1	4-GE301B	26″	All in active service in 1948.	
$24,200	42,000	Brill 99ER-1	4-WH1433	26″	All in active service in 1948.	Last cars built by J.G. Brill Co.
$6,500	46,000	Brill 77E-1 (later Brill 27MCB-3X)	4-GE203L	33″	All in active service in 1948.	Built 1917-1918 for Philadelphia Rapid Transit Co. as Nos. 4024, 4045 and 4106.

Roster of Snowplows and Sweepers

Car No.	Type	Size	Year Acquired	Builder	Disposition	Notes
Unknown	Wedge	Single-truck	7/95	Unknown	Scrapped 1899.	Steam-powered plow acquired with steam dummies. It was probably never used.
1	Rotary	Double-truck	1910	Smith & Wallace	Scrapped 1940.	Last used in 1922.
2	Rotary	Single-truck	1899	Ruggles	Scrapped in late 1930s.	Originally No. 1.
3	Wedge	Single-truck	1899	Brill	Scrapped in late 1930s.	
1	Sweeper	Single-truck	1899	McGuire	Scrapped in late 1930s.	
2	Sweeper	Single-truck	1902	McGuire	Scrapped in late 1940s.	
3	Sweeper	Single-truck	1912	McGuire	Scrapped in late 1940s.	
4	Sweeper	Double-truck	1922	McGuire-Cummings	Still in active service.	Cost $4,000.
5	Sweeper	Double-truck	1940	Russell	Still in active service.	Acquired secondhand; was New York State Railway's No. 3014; built 1918. Received trucks from No. 43.
34	Plow	Double-truck	1914	Jewett	Scrapped in 1941.	Former passenger car No. 34; converted to snowplow about 1930.

Roster of Milk, Freight and Work Cars

Car No.	Type	Size	Year Acquired	Builder	Disposition	Notes
1	Work	Single-truck	1896	Brill	Scrapped about 1914.	Later renumbered to No. 5.
1	Milk	Single-truck	1897	P&WCT	Date of scrapping unknown.	Built from body of a steam dummy.
1	Sprinkler	Double-truck	1899	Taunton	Scrapped about 1918.	
01	Milk/Freight	Single-truck	1899	Jackson & Sharp	Scrapped 1925.	Originally milk car No. 1; converted to freight service and renumbered in 1909.
02	Work/Freight	Single-truck	1896	Lamokin	Sold 1926.	Originally passenger car No. 4; rebuilt to work car No. 02 in 1902.
03	Work	Single-truck	1902	Brill	Scrapped about 1911.	
04	Work/Freight	Double-truck	1903	Brill	Scrapped in late 1940s.	Double cab motored flat car.
05	Work/Freight	Double-truck	1909	St. Louis	Scrapped in late 1940s.	Double cab motored flat car.
06	Milk	Double-truck	1909	Jewett	Sold 1925.	
07	Work/Freight	Double-truck	1911	Jewett	Remains in active service as line car.	
08	Freight	Double-truck	1918	Brill	Sold 1925 to Sand Springs Railway.	Refrigerated freight motor.
6	Work	Single-truck	1896	Brill	Scrapped about 1933.	Former passenger car No. 6; converted to emergency car in 1907.
8	Work	Double-truck	1898	Jackson & Sharp	Scrapped 1933.	Former passenger car No. 8; converted to work car about 1912.
14	Work	Double-truck	1902	Brill	Scrapped 1926.	Former passenger car No. 14; converted to emergency car in 1914.
16	Work	Double-truck	1902	Brill	Scrapped 1922.	Former passenger car No. 16; converted to line car in 1914.
17	Work	Double-truck	1906	Brill	Scrapped about 1933.	Former passenger car No. 17; converted to emergency car in 1926.
1-5	Ballast car	Single-truck	1898	Jackson & Sharp	Unknown.	Acquired for construction of West Chester line. Carried coal to Ridley Creek Powerhouse.
—	Flat car	Double-truck	1948	Unknown.	Remains in active service.	Nonpowered car. Originally built for Pennsylvania Railroad. Sold to Philadelphia and Western Railway in 1908. Sold to PST in 1948. Trucks from No. 05.

Index

Philadelphia & Wes[t]

CON[NECTING]

AT SIXTY-NINTH STREET TERMINAL WITH

Allow thirty minutes from Market Street Ferries and twenty minutes from Broad Street

| Highland Park | Newtown Square | ■ ■ | Llanerch | Oakmont |
| Manoa | West Chester | | Brookline | Ardmore |

| DAILY, INCLUDING SUNDAY | | **WEST CHESTER DIVISION** | | | SCHEDULE SUBJECT TO CHANG[E] |

WESTWARD

Dist.	STATIONS	AM	AM	AM	AM		PM	PM	PM	PM	AM	AM	PM	PM	PM	PM	AM	AM	AM	STATIO[NS]
0.00	**Sixty-ninth St. Term.**	.....	.....	.....	5.30		10.00	10.30	11.00	11.30	12.00	12.30	1.03	1.08	1.14	1.20	1.23	1.38	1.44	**Sixty-ninth St**
0.59	State Road	.....	.....	.....	5.32	And	10.02	10.32	11.02	11.32	12.02	12.32	1.05	1.10	1.16	1.22	1.25	1.40	1.46	State Road
1.09	Highland Park	.....	.....	.....	5.34	half-hourly	10.04	10.34	11.04	11.34	12.04	12.34	1.08	1.13	1.19	1.25	1.28	1.43	1.49	Highland Par
1.65	Kirklyn	.....	.....	.....	5.36	thereafter	10.06	10.36	11.06	11.36	12.06	12.36	1.10	1.15	1.21	1.27	1.30	1.45	1.51	Kirklyn
2.05	Llanerch	4.38	4.53	5.08	5.37	until	10.07	10.37	11.07	11.37	12.07	12.37	1.12	1.17	1.23	1.29	1.32	1.47	1.53	Llanerch
2.92	Manoa	4.41	4.56	5.11	5.41	10.00 p.m.	10.11	10.41	11.11	11.41	12.11	12.41								Manoa
3.30	Eagle	4.42	4.57	5.12	5.42		10.12	10.42	11.12	11.42	12.12	12.42								Eagle
4.82	**Brookthorpe Hills**	4.46	5.01	5.16	5.46		10.16	10.46	11.16	11.46	12.16	12.46								**Brookthorpe H**
5.63	Broomall	4.49	5.04	5.19	5.49		10.19	10.49	11.19	11.49	12.19	12.49								Broomall
6.51	Larchmont	4.52	5.07	5.22	5.52		10.22	10.52	11.22	11.52	12.22	12.52								Larchmont
7.34	Ashley	4.54	5.09	5.24	5.54		10.24	10.54	11.24	11.54	12.24	12.54								Ashley
7.77	**Newtown Square**	4.56	5.11	5.26	5.56		10.26	10.56	11.26	11.56	12.26	12.56								**Newtown Squ**
8.43	Kirks	4.58	5.13	5.28	5.58	15-minute	10.28	10.58	11.28	11.58	12.28	12.58								Kirks
9.43	Florida Park	5.00	.....	5.30	6.00	service will	10.30	.....	11.30	.....	12.30	.....								Florida Park
10.08	Castle Rock	5.02	.....	5.32	6.02	be main-	10.32	.....	11.32	.....	12.32	.....								Castle Rock
10.62	Edgemont	5.03	.....	5.33	6.03	tained on	10.33	.....	11.33	.....	12.33	.....								Edgemont
11.39	Penn Hotel	5.05	.....	5.35	6.05	Saturdays,	10.35	.....	11.35	.....	12.35	.....								Penn Hotel
11.92	**Gradyville Road**	5.07	.....	5.37	6.07	Sundays	10.37	.....	11.37	.....	12.37	.....								**Gradyville Ro**
12.76	Street Road	5.09	.....	5.39	6.09	and Holi-	10.39	.....	11.39	.....	12.39	.....								Street Road
13.32	Willistown	5.10	.....	5.40	6.10	days when	10.40	.....	11.40	.....	12.40	.....								Willistown
14.57	Chester Road	5.13	.....	5.43	6.13	necessary.	10.43	.....	11.43	.....	12.43	.....								Chester Road
15.64	**East Milltown**	5.15	.....	5.45	6.15		10.45	.....	11.45	.....	12.45	.....								**East Milltown**
16.74	Goshen Church	5.18	.....	5.48	6.18		10.48	.....	11.48	.....	12.48	.....								Goshen Chur
17.97	Chatwood	5.22	.....	5.52	6.22		10.52	.....	11.52	.....	12.52	.....								Chatwood
19.10	**West Chester**	5.27	.....	5.57	6.27		10.57	.....	11.57	.....	12.57	.....								**West Chester**

EASTWARD

Dist.	STATIONS	AM	AM	AM	AM	AM	AM	AM	AM	AM		PM	PM	PM	PM	AM	AM	AM	STATIO[NS]
0.00	**West Chester**	.....	.....	.....	.....	.....	.....	.....	5.30			10.30	.....	11.00	.....	12.00	.....	1.00	**West Chester**
1.13	Chatwood								5.35			10.35	.....	11.05	.....	12.05	.....	1.05	Chatwood
2.36	Goshen Church								5.38			10.38	.....	11.08	.....	12.08	.....	1.08	Goshen Chur
3.46	**East Milltown**								5.41	And half-hourly		10.41	.....	11.11	.....	12.11	.....	1.11	**East Milltown**
4.53	Chester Road								5.43	thereafter until		10.43	.....	11.13	.....	12.13	.....	1.13	Chester Road
5.78	Willistown								5.45	10.30 p.m.		10.45	.....	11.15	.....	12.15	.....	1.15	Willistown
6.84	Street Road								5.46			10.46	.....	11.16	.....	12.16	.....	1.16	Street Road
7.18	**Gradyville Road**								5.48			10.48	.....	11.18	.....	12.18	.....	1.18	**Gradyville Ro**
7.71	Penn Hotel								5.50			10.50	.....	11.20	.....	12.20	.....	1.20	Penn Hotel
8.48	Edgemont								5.52			10.52	.....	11.22	.....	12.22	.....	1.22	Edgemont
9.02	Castle Rock								5.53			10.53	.....	11.23	.....	12.23	.....	1.23	Castle Rock
9.67	Florida Park								5.55			10.55	.....	11.25	.....	12.25	.....	1.25	Florida Park
10.67	Kirks						5.28		5.58			10.58	11.13	11.28	11.58	12.28	12.58	1.28	Kirks
11.33	**Newtown Square**						5.30		6.00	15-minute service will		11.00	11.15	11.30	12.00	12.30	1.00	1.30	**Newtown Squ**
11.76	Ashley						5.31		6.01	be maintained on		11.01	11.16	11.31	12.01	12.31	1.01	1.31	Ashley
12.59	Larchmont						5.34		6.04	Saturdays, Sundays		11.04	11.19	11.34	12.04	12.34	1.04	1.34	Larchmont
13.47	Broomall						5.37		6.07	and Holidays when		11.07	11.22	11.37	12.07	12.37	1.07	1.37	Broomall
14.28	**Brookthorpe Hills**						5.40		6.10	necessary.		11.10	11.25	11.40	12.10	12.40	1.10	1.40	**Brookthorpe H**
15.80	Eagle						5.44		6.14			11.14	11.29	11.44	12.14	12.44	1.14	1.44	Eagle
16.18	Manoa						5.45		6.15			11.15	11.30	11.45	12.15	12.45	1.15	1.45	Manoa
17.05	Llanerch	*4.41	4.50	*5.05	*5.11	5.20	5.27	*5.35	5.49	6.19		11.19	11.33	11.49	12.19	12.49	1.18	1.48	Llanerch
17.45	Kirklyn	*4.43	4.52	*5.07	*5.13	5.22	5.29	*5.37	5.50	6.20		11.20	.....	11.50	12.20	12.50	.....	.....	Kirklyn
18.01	Highland Park	*4.45	4.54	*5.09	*5.15	5.24	5.31	*5.39	5.52	6.22		11.22	.....	11.52	12.22	12.52	.....	.....	Highland Par
18.51	State Road	*4.47	4.56	*5.11	*5.17	5.26	5.33	*5.41	5.54	6.24		11.24	.....	11.54	12.24	12.54	.....	.....	State Road
19.10	**Sixty-ninth St. Term.**	*4.50	4.59	*5.14	*5.20	5.29	5.36	*5.44	5.56	6.26		11.26	.....	11.56	12.26	12.56	.....	.....	**Sixty-ninth St**

* Not run on Sundays and Holidays.

Names of Stations which are fare limits in heavy-faced type.

CONNECTING LINES

For Darby, Holmes, Folsom, Morton and Swarthmore change at Collingdale via Parker Avenue.

For Darby, Glenolden, Moore, Norwood, Ridley Park, Eddystone, Chester, Marcus Hook and Wilmington change at Sharon Hill via Chester Pike.

For Kennett Square, Avondale and West Grove change at West Chester.

For Downingtown, Coatesville and Lancaster change at West Chester.

For Bryn Mawr, Wayne, Strafford, Norristown, Allentown, Bethlehem and Water Gap change at 69th Street Terminal.

For Rates, Special Cars, etc., write Superintendent Transportatio[n]
Upper Darby, Pa.

WEE[K] WEST[WARD]

Dist.	STATIONS	AM	AM	AM	AM	AM
0.00	Sixty-ninth St. Terminal	.....	5.26	5.41	5.56	6.11	6.2[6]
0.59	State Road	.....	5.28	5.43	5.58	6.13	6.2[8]
1.09	Highland Park	.....	5.31	5.46	6.01	6.16	6.3[1]
1.65	Kirklyn	.....	5.33	5.48	6.03	6.18	6.3[3]
2.05	Llanerch	5.20	5.35	5.50	6.05	6.20	6.3[5]
2.85	Brookline	5.24	5.39	5.54	6.09	6.24	6.3[9]
3.59	Oakmont	5.26	5.41	5.56	6.11	6.26	6.4[1]
4.26	Ardmore Junction	5.28	5.43	5.58	6.13	6.28	6.4[3]
5.31	Ardmore	5.33	5.48	6.03	6.18	6.33	6.4[8]

EAST[WARD]

Dist.	STATIONS	AM	AM	AM	
0.00	Ardmore	.....	.....	5.37	And	6.
1.05	Ardmore Junction	.....	.....	5.42	quarter-	6.
1.72	Oakmont	.....	.....	5.44	hourly	6.
2.45	Brookline	.....	.....	5.46	thereafter	7.
3.26	Llanerch	5.20	5.35	5.50	until	7.
3.66	Kirklyn	5.22	5.37	5.52	6.52 a.m.	7.
4.22	Highland Park	5.24	5.39	5.54		7.
4.72	State Road	5.26	5.41	5.56		7.
5.31	Sixty-ninth St. Terminal	5.29	5.44	5.59		7.